COLLECTING
for Fun and Profit

COLLECTING
for Fun and Profit

Mel Lewis

PROTEUS
London & New York

PROTEUS BOOKS is an imprint of
the Proteus Publishing Group

United States
PROTEUS PUBLISHING COMPANY, INC.
733 Third Avenue New York, N.Y. 10017

distributed to the trade by:
THE SCRIBNER BOOK COMPANIES, INC.
597, Fifth Avenue
New York, N.Y. 10017

United Kingdom
PROTEUS (PUBLISHING) LIMITED
Bremar House,
Sale Place,
London, W2 1PT.

ISBN 0 906071 23 2 (h/b)
       0 906071 23 2 (p/b)

First published in US 1981
First published in UK 1981
Printed and bound in England
by Butler & Tanner Ltd.

Contents

DEDICATION

To my mother

Let me thank the editor of Art & Antiques Weekly magazine for giving a journalist a break, the opportunity, ten years ago, of becoming a fulltime antique and collecting nutcase. My gratitude is due, too, to Tony Gill, expert on overseas trading, Franklin's Camberwell Antique Market, for a free run of their stands, pictorially speaking; also to the Press officers of the key London and American auction houses. Gill Colver, my personal assistant, helped me put this book together, stopped me making a fool of myself grammatically and otherwise, and proved beyond all shadow of doubt, that the IBM Executive is mightier than the fountain pen.

Photographs were supplied by the following:-
Mel Lewis
Ray Gaffney
Christie's, London
Sotheby, Parke Bernet & Co., New York
Sotheby's, London
Messrs: Sotheby, King & Chasemore — The Pulborough Saleroom

Introduction

I have a hankering to create the smallest collection in the world. It would consist of the names of all those who collect nothing at all. At the last count there were a mere 50,000,000 collectors worldwide. But what about all those who are still too shy to admit to collecting artificial eyes, cruet sets, photographs of Siamese twins, old shoes, oily engine rags, clothes hangers? To all of you I say: be brave. Own up! There's nothing to be ashamed of. We accept you. Oh, and by the way, your collectable is already old hat (in fact old hats, especially *chapeaux melons*—the good old British bowler—and top hats are a current fad with the chic Parisiens), so much so that, likely as not, there is already a club devoted to just your secret passion.

Nothing is an exclusive preserve of the ingenious collector; not anymore. Anything that could be—and surely was—included in the past is now just as surely collected. Because whatever anyone can laugh at today, tomorrow becomes a prime target for those gifted with lateral thinking ability otherwise know as collectors' chutzpah.

In this book I have tried to stick fairly faithfully to items whose cost will not force the newcomer to collecting to mortgage his soul, or even his home. There are plenty of low-priced opportunities for the shrewd collector. The history of this particular pastime is strewn with examples of items that we consider trash one day, only to be feverishly sought after a couple of years later. If I do stray it's because bargains are still around waiting to be picked up and trading up is still the name of this game.

To be honest, I have a few ideas for collectables not featured in this volume, but kept up my capacious sleeve ready to be passed on when and only when I have cornered the market.

That said, I will spotlight what I take to be the best news yet for collectors with a do-it-yourself turn of mind: make your own collectables.

If you do, you won't be the first here, either. For one Sotheby's furniture director left his comfortable saleroom post to devote himself to making netsuke, Japanese belt toggles in intricate shapes. And guess what: his boxwood and horn animal-carved netsuke are a sell-out sucess at every one-man exhibition he holds.

Mel Lewis 1980

1
Ephemera: Something For Next To Nothing

What is ephemera? No definition satisfies *every* ephemerist. But there is a "groundsheet" consensus that an item can correctly be described as ephemera (the singular, *ephemeron*, is never used) if it is two-dimensional, printed or hand written, and was made to be discarded. Ephemera is therefore usually paper, though printed handkerchiefs and even metal badges may qualify. The ephemerist also glosses happily over the fact that cigarette cards were produced to be collected, i.e. kept, from an early date in their history, and that old carved playing cards will see most of us out - and welcomes such items into the ranks of ephemera.

Even without these tobacco adjuncts, the list would be formidable, including, as it does: greeting cards, menus, timetables, posters, legal documents, trade cards, letterheads, postcards, stocks and shares, packaging, labels, theater programs, tickets, letters, bookmarks, bookplates, jeans labels, I.O.U.s, rejection slips, business stationery, parking tickets, dance cards, betting slips, and a hundred other flimsy relics.

The ephemerist recognizes three rough groups of ephemera, the transient such as a bus ticket; the semi-durable—like a passport, and the "everlasting"—a commemorative. The specialist may go for nothing but printed letterheads or mourning cards; but the collector who follows a theme, such as aviation history, will be delighted to give shelf space to the odd cigarette card on ballooning, or an unused air ticket from a flight that crashed, or the map used on a famous flight.

Stocks and Shares - Scripophily

"DO NOT DESTROY SEEMINGLY WORTHLESS SECURITIES. Submit them to us—they may have value". The advice offered in a headline blurb as part of the publicity of R.M. Smythe & Co. Inc. of New York is certainly worth taking seriously. Collectable stocks and shares (scripophily) form what is probably the most lively and fastest-appreciating area right now. Over a 17-month period stretching from March 1978 to July 1979 the retail value of selected Chinese bonds increased by over 1500 per cent. Similarly, over the same period, Russian railway bonds improved in value by over 640 per cent, and Russian cities, over an 11-month period from August 1978 to August 1979 were 400 per cent better off. Bonds were neglected for years probably because people assumed that, like stamps, they were issued in thousands or even millions. Some were, but like stamps, many have disappeared and some that remain are rarities. Today's "penny blacks" of the bond world are Chinese, Russian and American Confederate bonds.

The financial history of the modern world is riddled with instances of governments reneging on the debts of a regime they have ousted, usually by revolution. Lenin warned investors against buying bonds to finance the expansion of Russian cities in the 1900s. He promised that come the revolution they would become worthless paper, and kept his word. In China, war with Japan delayed repayment on western funded municipal and railway expansion schemes and the Communist government under Mao Tse-Tung similarly defaulted.

The debt contracted by the Confederate States of America was likewise repudiated following their defeat in 1865: the government of the victorious United States refused to pay. The 14th amendment to the constitution, passed in June 1866 enacts that "the United States, or any single state, shall not take over or pay any debt or liability contracted for purpose of supporting the insurrection or rebellion against the United States".

In the 1860s the Confederate Congress raised vast amounts of money

A $1,000 bearer bond issued in Richmond on April 1, 1864
by the Confederates.

to bolster the Confederate cause in the War of Secession. Confederate bonds are among the most desirable today. Colorful curiosities in bonds and shares abound: the Cotton Loan bond of January 29, 1863, a Confederate issue, was "tri-valued at: 1,000 pounds Sterling–2,500 French francs–4,000 pounds of cotton". You could actually trade in this issue for bale after bale of real cotton. Russian governments issued certificates to fund municipal schemes and railway expansion.

It helps to know how bonds differ from shares. Bonds, the most popular, are loans secured by assets and issued by governments and companies. Bonds are the picturesque certificates, watermarked, and of heavy paper; the engravings, where they appear are, as with banknotes, of fine quality and depth. The pictures vividly indicate the business for which they were issued: thus there are trains, ships, mining scenes, and so on. The first company set up on a joint-stock basis dates back to the 16th century. By far the greatest volume of company issues dates to the 19th century when the first railway companies were started up. The British Stockton & Darlington Railway Company was established in 1825 as the first public railway and the first steam railway. Massachusetts inaugurated its first railway two years later, and all told, in the United States, 9,000 separate railway companies were formed. Henry Wells and William Fargo set up the American Express Company in 1850. With no established parcel post service, private companies established themselves to convey goods, valuables and money quickly and safely.

When Wells and Fargo set up their unincorporated association, capitalised at a mere $150,000, each shareholder was personally liable for any company losses — a point which helped emphasize the company's probity and outstanding record.

One cute rider to the articles of association was that the shares could not be bought without approval of the board of directors or be sold to "married women, infants or irresponsible persons". Some 40 years later William Fargo's younger brother, James Congdell could write to the manager of his new Paris branch: "When the day comes that American Express has to hire a female employee it will close its doors!".

Most bonds are "bearer": they do not feature the name of the investor and can be passed on by the owner to someone else. A bond will state, in several languages, the terms of the loan including the amount of capital, the bank upon which it was drawn, the denomination and the interest payable to the bondholder. Coupons are attached to bonds and these were cut off as the interest was paid at pre-arranged dates. Bonds tend to be more picturesque than share certificates. The owner of shares in a company owns a specific portion of its net assets and shares in a proportion of the profits. A certificate will show the name and address of the investor with the serial number and denomination. Signed bonds carry a cachet in today's market. Look for names like J.D. Rockefeller, J. Paul Getty, Wells and Fargo, or one-time London City whizzkid Jim Slater. The name of Hugh Hefner, of Playboy Enterprises, is also desirable, but not nearly as much as the vignetted engravings that feature on some of his early issues. Apparently the earlier a Playboy certificate, the sexier the vignette.

Famous frauds, swindles and failures are vividly encapsulated in bond and share certificates, which go right back to the South Sea Bubble fiasco of the early 1700s. When Rolls Royce went under its shares were available for pennies, but today they are fetching £100 to £150 ($250 to $375) each. The failure of Berni Cornfeld's Investors Overseas Service (IOS) has turned today into a minor success story for those who have acquired some of its shares.

Bonds, being decorative, are often framed; they look fine in the board-room or office—especially if your company is doing better than the busted business on the wall! Low numbers (1 - 100) in bond issues carry a premium, and if it can be discovered who owned a share certificate, from its number, this, too, could enhance value. The more immediately enjoyable aspect of the hobby is the visual appeal: even the railwayana fan can thrill to the sight of a great loco with massive cow-catcher attached (accurately engraved) steaming through a scenic part of its route.

Literature for the scripophily specialist is still pretty thin on the ground, but getting better. Many of the dealers put out occasional catalogs of their stock, with prices. Given the volatile state of the market, a constantly updated literature, such as catalogs afford, offers a more accurate pulse on the market. R.M. Smythe of New York publish a five-issue-a-year magazine called Friends of Financial History; inside is a collectors' shopping guide giving a quick run-down of scripophily dealers around the world, listing their specialities. The firm also does postal auctions, operates a bourse and publishes the Robert D. Fisher Manuals of Valuable and Worthless Securities, in hard cover and microfilm.

Here are some of the books worth looking into: Criswell, Grover C., *Confederate and Southern State Bonds*, Criswell's (USA), 1961, revised 1980; Drumm U. and Henseler, A., *Chinesische Anleihen und Aktien*, Freunde Historische Wertpapiere (Germany), 1976; Drumm, U. and Henseler, A., *Old Securities, Russian Railway Bonds*, Freunde Historische Wertpapiere (Germany), 1975; 2nd ed. 1979; Hendy, Robin, *Collecting Old Bonds and Shares*, Stanley Gibbons, 1978; Narbeth, Colin, Hendy, Robin, Stocker, Christopher, *Collecting Paper Money and Bonds*, Cassell, 1979.

These are the main dealers and their addresses worldwide: R.M. Smythe & Company Inc., 'Old Securities', 170 Broadway, New York, NY 10038, USA; T. Isler, Edison Strasse 10, CH-8050, Zurich, Switzerland; F. Kuhlmann, Seiler Strasse 15-17, 3000 Hanover 1,

West Germany; F.M. Sutor, Luetzow Strasse 78, 5650 Solingen 1, West Germany; Spink & Son, 5-7 King Street, London, SW1; Herzog Hollender Phillips & Company, 9 Old Bond Street, London, W1; Non Valeurs, "KNYSNA", Redricks Lane, Harlow, Essex; The London Scripophily Centre Limited, 5 Albemarle Street, London W1; The St. James's Collection, 28/30 Chiltern Street, London, W1; Belcher Associates, 352 Grand Buildings, Trafalgar Square, London WC2; Stanley Gibbons, 395 Strand, London, WC2.

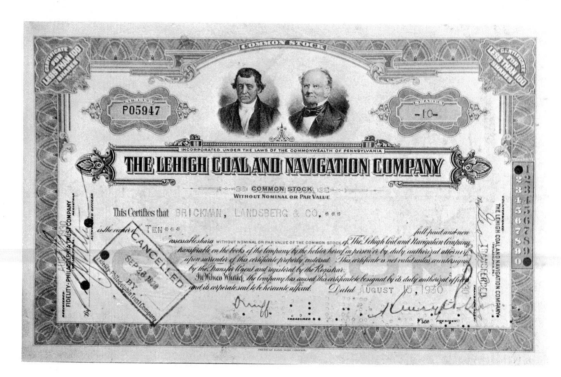

Theater mementoes

Noel Coward said that the best souvenirs are memories. But the collector of theater ephemera—theatricalia or theater memorabilia are other clumsier names for the same activity—demands more tangible evidence of pleasurable moments gone by. He'll collect every scrap of paper or flimsy relic related to his favorite subject, hoarding cigarette cards depicting actors and actresses, costume designs, newspaper reviews, posters, postcards, scripts, photographs, props and scenery, theater tickets—even the account books from theaters or music halls.

Perhaps most treasured of all are autographs. But not all personalities gave them. George Bernard Shaw often refused to pick up a pen but would offer to answer questions. Noel Coward first demanded a donation—even a token one—to the Actors' Orphanage which he headed for many years. Ivor Novello used to have his dresser "ghost" his signature on fan photographs and one comedy star always put "sincerely" over his name after someone had once mischievously inserted "I.O.U. £10" above it.

Designs for stage sets and costumes are the most sought-after and highly priced of all theater relics. The work may be in gouache, watercolor or pencil. Picasso, Braque and Bakst are among the many artistic innovators who gave their services to the theater and ballet after the turn of the century. These were real working drawings and often bear the written instructions to the seamstress or scene-builder, all of which add to the fascination. Cuttings relating to early showings of now famous stars and performers are much in demand, as are photographs of actors, especially those known as "front-of-house" stills, the pictures displayed by the entrance to the theater and encased in glass to lure you inside. The first programs were small playbills or posters. Some were pasted up and others sold to the theatergoers: posters advertising plays boldly featuring top actors of the past are not easy to find. But you may discover their names at the foot of a more inconsequential cast list, from an era before they hit the big time.

Theater programs proper date from the mid-19th century. The best ones are those distributed on the First Night. You get a useful potted history of playwrights and artistes—as well as an extra bonus in the form of the ads for products, restaurants and services to be found, often, close by the playhouse.

This autograph was sold at auction recently for £260 ($620).

Cigarette cards and silks

The first cigarette cards were quite blank. Their function was to stiffen the flimsy paper pack and stop the cigarettes inside getting crushed. America first exploited picture cards as a sales gimmick in the 1870s. W.D. & H.O. Wills followed suit for Britain in 1885. As soon as the American Tobacco Company had ousted its main rivals and obtained a monopoly in the United States the company no longer felt the desperate need to outdo the competition with attractive extras. But British manufacturers kept up the good work.

Cigarette cards captured the public imagination from the start, in the days before cinema or TV, and the reproduction of photographs (which was not widespread until the Twenties). Many collectors go for Ogden's Guinea Golds, genuine little photographs dating from 1897 to 1907. More than 26,000 subjects were covered, offering a fascinating window on to what people looked like at the turn of the century.

People who collect militaria, sporting antiques, painting and pottery, music hall fans, and many others often keep a small collection of cards on their favorite topic for quick reference. The backs of cigarette cards are usually crammed with nutshell knowledge and useful facts about the subject on the front.

The paper shortage at the beginning of the last war saw the end of the thriving cigarette card industry. Today's collector shuns creased or grubby cards and those that have been stuck into a scrap book, so spoiling the rich vivid colors that are often finer than anything a modern printer can aspire to.

Without paper, firms issued pictures printed on (or woven into) rectangles of fine silk. Whatever one's interest there was a silk series to complement it. The American Tobacco Company dared to bring out a run of Bathing Girls and Actresses, Maps and Flowers, Presidents, Famous Queens, Women of Ancient Egypt and many others. Phillips tempted smokers with Moths, War Leaders, Heraldry, Old Masters, VC Heroes, Clan Tartans, Birds of the Tropics. From Australia came Butterflies, Flowers and Queens. South African Flowers, Regimental Uniforms of Canada and Irish Patriots can all be found on silk, while woven silks were a Dutch speciality. The years 1912-19 are the key years of the silk, with Godfrey Phillips, the tobacco firm, leading the field. Phillips produced a vast variety of subjects on big silk - 165mm x 120mm. The American

Tobacco Company produced even larger examples and Carrera issued the biggest silks of all: 305mm x 208mm, but many silks are roughly the same size as the standard cigarette card. Hand painting on bleached silk began with the ancient Chinese. It was probably Thomas Stevens of Coventry who started the vogue in Britain in the 19th century. But it was in magazines, not cigarette packs, that the first silks appeared, as a sales gimmick. The Gentlewoman contained a picture series entitled "The Gentlewoman of 100 Years Ago" from 1890. Floral Beauties and Soldiers of the King were free giveaways at a later date with copies of My Weekly. Lea, a tobacco manufacturer of Stockport, introduced silks after 1902, one set of 30 showing butterflies and moths; then came Old Pottery. His Regimental Crests and Badges was probably issued at the outbreak of the Great War to cash in on the chauvinistic hysteria that was sweeping the country.

Today's collector is saddened by the harsh treatment meted out by earlier aficionados. If silks weren't screwed up or tied in little bundles or stashed in damp boxes (which led to foxing, a fungus which shows itself in tiny brown dots) they were mutilated in other ways. A favorite female pastime was to sew the attractive silks into cushions, screens and tablecloths. Some paper-backed silks were soaked in water to remove the glued-on paper, then dried in a hot oven. No wonder then that an impeccable set of 50 silks is a plum collector's prize today.

Playing-cards

American souvenir cards, mostly put out by the U.S. Playing Card Co., showing vignetted picturesque places, were a popular vogue from 1893 to 1916.

De Luxe packs appeared with each card having nicely rounded corners; Perry & Co. made waterproof cards, and in Britain in 1874 a commemorative pack appeared in honor of the marriage of the Duke of Edinburgh. The court cards and aces bore portraits of Queen Victoria, President Grant and the Tsar.

Superior color printing techniques led to a rush of vividly produced cards celebrating actors and actresses, famous beauties, railways, and fanciful pin-ups: the Vargas pin-up pack sells for $250 or so (£100) and is well worth laying up as stock for capitalizing on at a later date.

Even fairly new novelty packs are much in demand, such as the American card pack which featured doctors, dentists, and nurses as the court figures. There are three intriguing political packs, issued

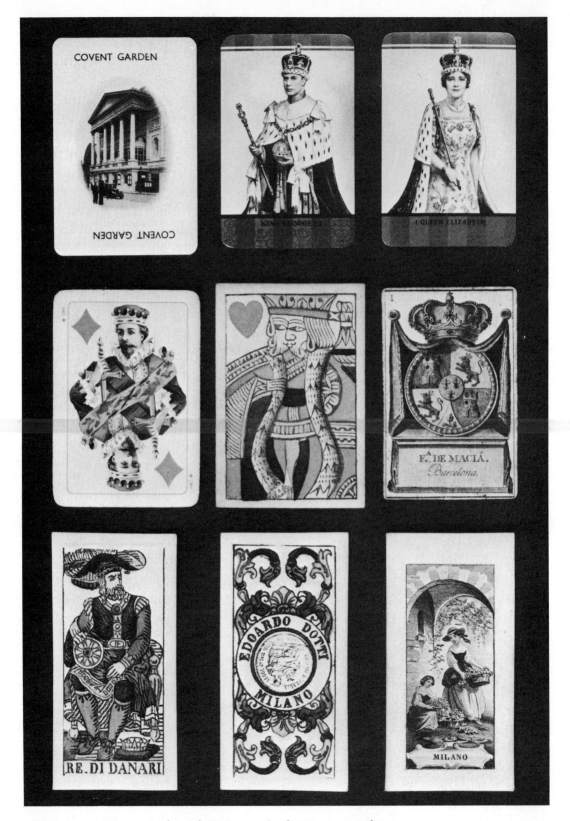

A selection of playing cards.

respectively in 1971, 1972 and 1973: Politicards (showing Nixon and his supporters, including Bob Hope), the President's Deck and the Executive Deck. The "President's Deck" depicts ex-President Nixon, his wife, and Spiro Agnew, with George Wallace and Hubert Humphrey as jokers. For a 1963 pack decorated with portraits of President Kennedy you could now pay $60 (£25).

The history of playing cards is a curious and grim one.

In c.1392 the treasurer to King Charles V1 of France paid a certain M. Gringonneur, a painter, 56 Paris sous "for three games of cards in gold and in diverse colors ornamented with various devices". The game caught on fairly quickly in Britain but an Act of Parliament of 1463 banned foreign imports. Many of the earliest playing cards were destroyed by Cromwell and his Puritan followers who regarded them as sinful. But the game survived nonetheless, and eventually the British settled on a style of suits based on a French patterned pack which had originated in Rouen in the 14th century.

Today's collector does not expect to pick up cards from much before the 19th century. Before the middle of the 19th century cards carried full-length pictures of Kings and Queens, not the double-headed variety of today's packs. And not all collectors go for complete sets; some buy singles or specialize in jokers or aces, and so on. Bad luck and the ace of spades go hand-in-hand. Apparently before the 19th century there was a tax payable on packs of cards, and a special stamp — an elaborate design to deter forgers—was impressed on the ace of spades to show the tax had been paid. Anyone found guilty of forging the "Old Frizzle", as the design was known, was liable to have his nostrils slit, his ears lopped off, or be branded with a red-hot poker. So the grim connotation is understandable!

Tarot cards

The tarot pack is generally thought to have originated in Italy and to have travelled over Europe, carried by gypsies. There are many regional variations in the designs, though in some places the occult or fortune-telling connection is not known and the cards are used in a variety of innocuous games.

Even those who don't regard themselves as superstitious flinch at the sight of the tarot pack. For as well as 52 suited cards there are other, less familiar, picture cards, including 'The Hanged Man', 'Death', 'The Devil' and 'The Popess', the crude drawing and bold coloring

19

somehow heightening the dramatic impact. As the tarot pack has a "standard', or games playing function, and also a "non-standard" use, they are doubly interesting to the card connoisseur.

The Devil card from a modern Tarot of the Witches pack.

A typical tarot pack uses the Italian signs of Money, Cups, Swords and Batons. Instead of the usual three, there are four court cards: king, queen, knight and knave, plus 10 numerical (or pip) cards, from 2 to 10, with an ace. The trumps - also known as 'atouts' - are numbered 1 to 21, with the last, the Fool, left unnumbered. The curious designs almost certainly originated in the 14th century, but there is no evidence to support the once popular theory that they originated in ancient Egypt or were associated with a lost 'black art' - though the church, which abhorred gambling and the drunkenness that went with it, condemned tarot cards, calling them "The Devil's Picture Book".

The earliest tarot cards were all hand-painted by commissioned artists. Tarots did not come into general circulation until the introduction of wood-block printing in the 15th century. Old tarot cards have been discovered in the bindings of books; bookbinders used them to stiffen covers when paper was in short supply. Possibly the most beautiful tarots are those of German origin; the Germans were the first to use wood-block printing for their cards. The theory is that they travelled from Italy over the Brenner Pass. Hand-stencilled cards are also known and these date only up to around 1850; after that date printing in its modern form takes over.

Some collectors opt for just one type of card from different regions or eras. The Death card is a gruesome but common favorite. Others collect only single-ended tarots (the pattern normally is "the right way up" whichever way you hold it): late 19th century samples can be had for as little as $120 (£50) each. Cards were meant to be handled, so rarely come in mint condition. The tarot card collector deals with the hurdle by buying what he needs to make up his collection, then trades up to examples in better condition. At the end of 1979 Stanley Gibbons, the London stamp, coin, stocks and shares and playing card dealers and auctioneers, reported that prices for antique card packs had shot up in value over the year by 45 per cent. Tarot packs had seen a similar improvement, with an animal tarot pack printed by Meyer of Germany in 1820 selling for £500 ($1,250) as against £350 ($875). Game packs printed in the late 19th century had doubled in value; packs of Snap and Happy Families from the 1880s were fetching $50 (£20). Even modern packs were enjoying something of a boom; in 1976 playing cards caricaturing President Giscard d'Estaing were withdrawn in France for reasons of taste. These now go for around $50 (£20) a pack.

Story papers and comic strips

Once upon a time, a writer referred to collectors of early boys' papers as: "Gentle suburban men with long memories..." Now that interest has become the focal point of sociological studies, exhibition, glossy books, and a vigorous collecting market has sprung up. Every kind of youthful reading matter is collectable. There are the gloriously Gothic 19th century "bloods" or "penny dreadfuls", the earliest comic strips, and the boys' story papers. Today the hobby is rapidly changing, as early copies become scarce, so that it pays to keep up with current trends, and, better still, to spot them before they arrive.

A fairly recent development, promoted no doubt by the Pop Art movement of the Sixties, which recognized the picture strip as an important kind of folk art, is collecting comic strip books like *Superman, Weird, Batman, The Incredible Hulk* and *Tales of the Zombies*. These super-heroes, brilliantly drawn and vividly depicted in lurid primary colors are now fetching the highest prices of all. A copy of *Superman No.1*, published in 1938, sold to a collector for $2,000 (£830) in 1974. A Canadian one-time book dealer recalls how he'd unpacked a crate of junk when in walked a stranger and handed him five $20 bills for the comic wrapped around an old painting. It was a *Batman No. 1, 1939*. That dealer started trading in comics, not books. (Number ones of leading comics have been reprinted and the unwary can be caught out).

The good news for British collectors is that the thousands of American servicemen in Britain during the war recieved millions of comics sent from home. Many of these with their stout glossy covers must have been passed on to British children, so they're around somewhere...

Likewise Americans have been buying up early British boys' books for over 25 years, especially copies of *Boys' Own Paper* and *Chums*, and it is interesting to note that British juvenilia was available across the Atlantic as early as 1880. One interesting early story paper, *The Young Gentlemen's Magazine*, began and folded in 1877. Copies are now only to be found in the University libraries of Yale and Illinois. Americans have cottoned on to the fact that British boys' papers are a unique social document, reflecting the life, laughs and attitude of a bygone age. For example, boys' papers have often taken an easy route regarding prejudices. If a prejudice was popular it was worth plugging; and if it was funny, too, so much the better. I remember the strip comics I used to read. There I learned that every Italian had a formidable black moustache, wore an apron and sold ice-cream. All Germans wore monocles, uniforms, an Iron Cross and clicked their heels. One parody which can perhaps be forgiven was the mercilessly depicted Mussolini in issues of D.C. Thomson's *Beano*, dating from the Second World War. The Italian leader was described as: "Musso the Wop—He's a bigga da flop". As victory loomed, *Il Duce* lost his swagger and the character was dropped.

Humor sparked the first comic strips, among them Popeye, Little Orphan Annie, and Barney Google; spacemen (well before the moon landings) and cowboys came later. The Yellow Kid was first created in 1896, Buster Brown appeared in the New York *World* papers in 1902. King Comics and Tip Top Comics started up in 1936. Books appeared in the Forties based on hugely popular strip characters like Jungle Jim, Terry and the Pirates, and Li'l Abner. Movie stars like Gene Autrey were immortalized in the strips, too, as were sporting personalities like Joe Louis the boxer, and baseball ace Babe Ruth. The war inspired a new breed: heroes and spies, Boy Commandoes, Spy Smasher, Captain America among them.

Collectors go for "firsts" and also banned issues. In 1955 horror comics were seized when parents and teachers feared they might have an evil influence on young children. Certainly there were abuses, and these "terror" epics are now hoarded with relish by collectors who are too old to be shocked by anything - except, perhaps, the prices they have to pay for such exotica.

The collecting of earlier comic and story papers follows a different pattern. The nostalgia element is paramount, so that titles currently commanding the highest prices are what the buyers grew up on as boys. They're buying back a bit of their youth, it seems. Typically, a collector will aim to own a specimen copy of a "run" (an unbroken series) of his favorite publication.

The *Magnet* and its companion paper, *The Gem,* are the current cream of the "old" UK market. Earlier 19th century story papers are priced high, too, but not in proportion to their added age. Papers like *Adventure, Rover, Wizard* and *Hotspur* once followed hard on the heels of *Gem* and *Magnet* in popularity. The most sought-after *Magnets* are those with red covers. Blue and white issues are also known. The very first *Magnet* had a red cover and collectors should beware confusing with a genuine original the anniversary souvenir reprint that was published in 1958. It takes an expert to tell the difference.

One collector bought a selection of story papers from a trader who also dealt in early dolls. It seemed a good buy. But later that collector discovered that all the illustrations showing 19th century children's costume had been snipped out. Moral? Always look closely before you buy. Look, too, for bound copies of comics and story papers. An owner may have had his copies custom bound with hard boards back and front. That way all the pages were protected from tears and damp and all the covers are intact. Publisher-bound series, however, may have only the top original cover present. Presumably for reasons of economy, the covers of every other issue were omitted.

Look into History of Comic Strips by Couperie and Horn, for background; subscribe to Cohen's Official Guide to Comic Books, or the Buyers Guide, 15800 Route 84N, E. Moline, Illinois 61244, or chat to Danny Posner the owner of London's Vintage Magazine Shop, when he's next in New York or San Francisco presiding over his new USA ventures founded on a comic strip, book and ephemera stock reputedly worth seven million dollars.

Beer labels

To get started as a labologist—the proper name for the beer label collector—you don't even need to buy bottles of beer. Simply write to the brewers and ask them to send labels that haven't been stuck on bottles. Labeling of bottled products began as far back as the 17th century, and in 1756 a black and white label appeared on port. Beer probably did not get labeled until 1834. One of the earliest and most sought after of labels is the stopper label which fastened over the cork used to firmly plug the escape of carbon dioxide which forms naturally from beer's yeasts. The cork was further sealed with wax or a foil cap and wire. In 1872 the screw stopper was patented and 1892 saw the invention of the crown cap.

"Top straps" then appeared. Like stopper labels, they are smaller than side labels and, say enthusiasts, often inspired designers to heights of creativity through the sheer difficulty of producing something eye-catching and legible in such a confined space. War issue labels are also cherished, these being similarly small scale to conform with wartime economies. One British brewery, Ind Coope & Allsopp, even went as far as to specify the reason for the change: "Miniature label necessitated by War Conditions".

The first bottle labels were circular; then came oval-shaped labels. Each brewer rapidly tried to establish an instantly recognizable identity. The Pittsburgh, USA, brewers issued a bizarre series of labels for their "Old Frothingslosh Beer"; these featured funny faces or dotty messages such as "Teddibly Stout", "Champain", or "Schnopps". Labels depicting animals and birds – of both sorts – are also avidly collected. The more successful houses were quickly imitated. They weren't so much fakes as mimicry meant to mislead. Thus, the oval shape, buff color and serial numbers of Guinness have all been copied, as have the curious wavy lines on the Bass label - it resembles the "protectionist" background on bank cheques. Also looking remarkably like the Bass label were those issued by the brewer who signed himself, with a similar italic flourish, "Brass". The Bass brewery at Burton-on-Trent, England, boasts what must be a collector's dream: an album of 1,900 forgeries and copyright infringements.

Special occasions have provided ideal occasions for brewers to go to town with spectacular – and highly collectable – labels. Thus, in 1959 Guinness of Dublin celebrated its bicentenary with an Extra Stout label printed on gold foil. The back of the bottle carried a portrait of the founder, Arthur Guinness, and there was a gold neck slip.

Jubilees, royal marriages and coronations have all been recorded on labels. Labels commemorating the 1911 coronation of King George V, that of King George V1 in 1937, and Queen Elizabeth in 1953 are all now at a premium. Perhaps the saddest commemorative was that released in 1961 by the Tollemache & Cobbold Brook Street Brewery, Ipswich. The operation was winding down and the label bore the cryptic message, "Final Brew".

Much more fun is the label commissioned by the Pecheur Group in France from noted artist Jean Cocteau. The label, affixed to the company's "3 Etoiles" (stars) De Luxe Pale Ale, shows a Greek-type god and asterisk-shaped stars—plus the famous artist/writer's signature.

Advertising

While printing was still in its infancy, boldly lettered broadsheets (paper printed on one side only) were produced to be handed out and nailed up on the wall. The first illustrated advertisement is believed to be one that appeared in the *Faithful Scout* for April 2-9 1652. A splendid drawing of two vanished jewels was used along with a descriptive text. Another early ad showed that slavery, popularly thought to have been an American vice, was far from uncommon in the UK, as the January 20 1769 copy of the *Edinburgh Advertiser* shows:
"TO BE SOLD
A BLACK BOY, about 16 years of age, healthy, strong and well made, has had the Measles and Smallpox, can shave and dress a little and has been for these several years accustomed to serve a single gentleman both abroad and at home..."

The rapidly expanding sophisticated American economy soon came to appreciate that a picture is worth a thousand words—so they set

A wartime advertising poster.

about perfecting that picture. In 1847 11 million advertisements were placed in 2,000 American newspapers, and a vicious battle for sales began. Sandwich men appeared for the first time in New York and hand-painted posters were pasted up everywhere.

Many of the collectors of original promotional material—posters, stand-up counter cards, packaging, enamelled plates, and so on—are commercial artists themselves; they find in their forerunners' efforts inspiration for their own work. In barely five years, say the leading London emporium for advertising material, DoDo in Westbourne Grove, prices have doubled. A fairly boring tinplate sign will go for $10 to $30 (£4 to £12), but interesting and good condition examples creep closer to $250 (£100). Enamelled plates that stood outside shops are bound to show signs of weathering.

Unchipped, unrusted enamel plates are likely to be recent copies. A papier mache giant size replica of a Bovril jar might set you back $30 (£12); a larger than life-size box of matches, a point-of-sale display gimmick, will go for around $40 (£15).

Pear's advertising

Companies like Jaeger, Listerine, Coca-Cola, Guinness all produced distinctive advertising over the years: that's partly how they became the household names they are today. But few products can boast advertisements as distinctive as those for Pear's soap. There are beautifully illustrated handbills, posters, presentation plates, Pear's annuals—even a 10 centime piece stamped with the soap's name—to collect.

Pear's ads were the soft-sell masterpieces of the 19th and early 20th centuries. Actress Lily Langtry cheerfully allowed her endorsement of the product to used in advertising. Beneath a portrait of the star ran the legend: "Since using Pear's soap for the hands and complexion I have discarded all others". It was this ad that Britain's *Punch* magazine lampooned so successfully in 1884. A cartoon showed a bedraggled tramp, exquisitely drawn by Harry Furniss, writing a letter to the editor: "Two years ago I used your soap, since when I have used no other". Bubbles was the name given to a painting by the artist Sir John Everett Millais. It shows a chubby, rosy-cheeked curly angel of a little boy gazing skywards at the bubbles he has just blown with a clay pipe and soapy water in a bowl. Pear's greatist publicist, Thomas J. Barrat, acquired the artist's permission to use the illustration, with one vital alteration: the addition of a little cake of soap of a certain name by the boy's feet. Examples of the illustration are avidly sought today. In 1916 Pear's Annual featured another famous painting, Landseer's

"Sea horses" by Fred Morgan was used by Pear's in 1894.

Monarch of the Glen. Today the early plates and presentation prints that appeared in Pear's publications are eagerly sought.

Bookmarkers

The first advertising bookmarkers won a seedy reputation for the vivid colors and brash hard-sell claims they made for the products depicted. (A brightly colored card bookmark on a ribbon advertising the Galerie Orangerie Verlag of Germany is bound into my copy of the International Antiques Yearbook. As such a reference work is unlikely to be read through systematically, it must make better sense than a page advertisement which may only be seen by a fraction of purchasers). An interesting sideline, in 19th century advertisers would be a selection of markers from "the quack electric craze", which lasted from 1880 to 1900. Even fewer people then than now understood how electricity worked and of course only a handful had power in the home. Firms were quick to capitalize on the "magic" properties of the new invisible energy and produced electric toothbrushes (nothing new, you see), electric plasters, electric cigarettes and electric belts and corsets. It helped if there were authorities to endorse the large claims, like Professor G.J. Baker of the Electropathic Association, 12 East 14th Street, New York. Soaps, clothes, patent medicines, foods and more were all aggressively plugged, usually on stiff paper or thin card bookmarkers.

An earlier craze, before techniques of colorful mass printing (chromolithography) had been perfected, was the ribbon bookmarker, an idea which dates back at least as far as Tudor times. In 1584 Christopher Barker, Queen's Printer, gave Queen Elizabeth a fringed silk bookmarker. Bible-style bookmarkers, long thin streamers of silk ribbon which were bound into the spine at the top and protruded slightly below the page, were in everyday use until the First World War. Ribbon remnants would be decorated in the last century, often with simple messages of affection or devotion, little talismen of religious belief: "In God is our Trust", "Search the Scriptures", "Forget me not" and, "Let us with a gladsome mind praise the Lord for He is Kind"; these are common in the US and UK. Silk thread embroidery became a popular parlor craft, akin to the sampler fad of previous years.

Hand painted bookmarkers — especially if the artist had any talent — and cut paper markers are top-of-the-tree collectables. The paperworker borrowed the techniques of the silhouettist, reversing the shades to have intricate cut white paper against a dark ribbon background. The most famous and desirable woven silk markers are those by Thomas Stevens of Coventry, renowned for his Steven-graph pictures. Some Stevens silks carry a woven mark to show the date a particular design was registered. Religious devotion figured large in Stevens' range of 50 designs dating to 1862, but there were Christmas and birthday greetings markers, too. In 1861, following suit with Queen Victoria, Britain plunged into mourning after the death of her beloved husband Albert, and black bookmarkers are common. Commemorative Stevens' bookmarkers, like the one bearing a portait of George Washington issued as a souvenir for the Centennial Exposition at Philadelphia, in 1876, are pricey. Stevens, W.H. Grant of Coventry and William Grant, a Stevens protégé, all produced bookmark souvenirs for the 1893 World's Fair Columbia Exposition in Chicago. Travel firms, insurance companies and publishers were quick to realize the advertising potential in something so often handled as a bookmarker — especially as it could often be retained long after the medium of presentation had been discarded. ABC Cinemas produced a celluloid marker to drum up interest in the Warner Bros film *Rhapsody in Blue,* "The Jubilant Story of George Gershwin" (1945). Publishers used bookmarkers to advertise in word and picture their forthcoming books. As recently as 1962 a thumbnail profile of authoress Iris Murdoch, together with a portrait, was issued on a bookmarker by Chatto & Windus to mark the publication of *An Unofficial Rose.* Unusual shape bookmarkers, like the Christmas cracker design put out by Tom Smith in c. 1929, or the scented marker of New York parfumier C.H. Selick, or those with a little cut-out piece on top forming a "page flap" all add to the fun and value of a collection. Perhaps the most apt bookmarker to cap a collection for an aberrant reader like myself would be the British Royal Air Force Recruiting issue of 1970. It states pithily: "PLEASE DO NOT MARK YOUR PLACE BY TURNING DOWN THE CORNER OF A PAGE — USE THIS".

2
Playthings Of The Past

A low-priced start to a collection of interesting and unusual toys could be made with large tin cars which the Japanese made in the 1950s and 1960s. And it has been suggested that an avant garde collection could include nothing but Japanese toy spacecraft, robots, space stations, and so on, produced in the first (and last) flush of excitement at the start of the space program which culminated in Man on the Moon in July, 1969.

Toy cars date back to the turn of the century when Marklin, the German firm, introduced them into its catalog. By 1902 the Nuremburg maker Gebruder Bing had captured the market for quality metal toys. The best Bing models had steering that really worked, polished brass accessories and painting as fine as any coachwork. French toymakers also shied away from cheapness: their forte was the de luxe model. BB and CR were two firms that excelled in hand-painted coachwork; their tiny car seats were padded and covered in satin or kid, and if the model had a convertible top it would be in real leather.

Toys signed FM are from the hand of French toymaker Fernand Martin. His greatest creations were the barber with the difficult customer, the pianist and the lady in the bath-chair.

Some of the earliest tin-plate vehicles look like toys but were really meant for adults: they are cigarette boxes in disguise. Around the turn of the century approximations of a new De Dion, Panhard, Benz or Peugeot, around a foot long, were produced; the front half of the body lifts up to reveal the cigarettes and the driver's seat, often as not, hinges forward to give access to a box of matches.

In the early years of this century a certain Dr. King formed an unrivalled collection of Penny Toys. Guided by a simple rule - only toys which could be bought on the streets of London for 1d were included - he amassed 1,700 pieces. Nowadays, with tin toys fetching three- and even four-figure sums, the collector confines himself rigidly for fear of ending up with no collection at all—or a superb collection but no home!

Mechanical toys

The earliest toymakers were nothing if not ingenious. In the 1870s and 1880s use was made of the flywheel mechanism, as it was reliable and had few moving parts. The mechanism could either be set in motion by twirling a knob with the fingers or, more likely, a piece of string could be wrapped round it and then rapidly unwound, rather like starting an outboard motor. Math. Hess, a German firm known especially for its Hessmobil, a model tin-plate car, used a flywheel which enabled the vehicle to be propelled through reduction gears. Another quaint little gimmick which must have charmed many a youth of that era was the fact that the car needed to be cranked up before it would go. Schuco produced a BMW model which had a clockwork motor with clutch, a hand brake, four forward gears and one reverse.

There were steam, hot air powered and eventually clockwork powered models, too. The German maker Lehmann is especially well known for his clockwork models typified by the eccentric behavior of the characters depicted. Thus the Stubborn Donkey shows a clown driving a cart pulled by a donkey which constantly trots forward and then rears up. Another bizarre creature is the Lehmann Beetle , which trots along flapping its wings at an alarming rate; the Bucking Bronco attempts to throw its rider over its head; Quack-Quack is a toy duck pulling a basket full of bobbing ducklings. Lehmann delighted in really dotty pieces, like the frightened bride who jumps up and down while the groom, on a motor bike, pulls her along in a trailer; the car with four odd wheels that refuses to be driven in a straight line; the nurse bathing a naughty baby, and others too numerous to mention.

The firm's work is always clearly marked—not surprising when you consider the excellence of its products.

To keep prices down tin toy makers were adept at recycling materials; throwaway parts used in oil can manufacture became wheels on early model cars. Slot and tab fixing is the most common sort of joinery in cheap tin cars, the better models being soldered. It was no accident that toy cars were made of lightweight tin; there was a tax on weight, which resulted in American makers being penalized

33

on the world markets in spite of the fact that their cast iron toys were of the highest quality. This also explains why, with lightness paramount, the decoration, often in brilliant colors, was more important than the shape. Paper lithography, begun in 1895 offered manufacturers a cheap means of decorating their toys; previously everything had had to be hand-painted or stenciled. Once decoration was a simple mechanical task, it was possible to have ships and trains and cars which look identical but bore different names according to their various destinations. So a ship looking exactly the same could sell in one market labeled "Kaiser Wilhelm" and in another labeled "Edward V11". Importing one tin toy to America had a special problem; it was a beer wagon and would have been banned in the prohibition days and had to be renamed.

An early 20th century tinplate clockwork toy.

Inevitably the new World started its own toy industry, the best known maker being Edward Ives. The firm began in 1868 and carried the banner "Ives toys make happy boys". There was a rowing man, trains and dancing figures motivated by the hot air rising from a cooking stove. Weedon, another American name to note, manufactured ships, engines and fire engines. Hafner specialized in cars and trains.

Die-cast toys

Die-cast car models were mass produced after the First World War and have only recently come to the fore as collectors' pieces. The earliest examples have a dangerously high lead content, and were really quite unsafe for children to be playing with. Eventually an alloy of aluminum, magnesium and copper, know as Zamac (or Mazac) was developed. The Chicago firm of Dowst Brothers, operating under the name Tootsietoy, produced models mimicking the Model T Ford, Chevrolet and Buick. Frank Hornby, brains behind the UK firm of Meccano, announced in 1933 that he would be producing die-cast vehicles, too, and the following year advertised for sale the now world famous Dinky toys. Dinky toys were largely discontinued in the Second World War except for one model: a replica of a petrol tanker, painted grey and with the word POOL in white paint on the side; this was the Government name for rationed petrol. Today collectors go for Tootsietoy, Dinky and Solido die-cast models made before World War II as they are irreplaceable period pieces, prized and cherished out of all proportion to the original cost or purpose. Especially sought after are Dinky delivery vans of the Thirties, like those advertising "Oxo - Beef at its Best" or "The Manchester Guardian". Trade vans with original advertising material painted over are not worth anywhere near as much, and of course pristine original condition is what the connoisseur aims for.

Scale models

Scale models, genuine little replicas and handmade one-off models, perhaps put together by a dedicated amateur hobbyist or a professional model builder, appeal to the perfectionist collector. They were playthings of adults rather than children—or at least a rather mature young man with an interest in things mechanical and engineering. Among the most popular models are railways. The German firms of Carette, Marklin, Bing and English firms such as Hornby and Bassett-Lowke made superlative replicas of engines and rolling stock. Perhaps the best of these were those made by W.J. Bassett-Lowke; Edward Exley was noted for his scale model rolling

Silver scale model of Wilson's biplane.

stock; Bonds, a model company based in Leeds, is another important one as are Hamblings and Mills Brothers. The condition of model trains, especially the paintwork is of little concern to serious collectors although it does have a dramatic effect on the price. The general rule is not to attempt to clean up grubby models but to pay due respect to the wear and tear of age, and leave them alone. Tin-plate models, never meant to last much longer than the few weeks following Christmas Day, will have suffered the most—which helps explain why they are so much in demand in showroom condition in the saleroom. Model boats, which are some of the most exciting toys ever produced, are also among the rarest, not least because many of them, out on their first trial run, no doubt, ended up among the sticklebacks and tadpoles, never to be sighted again.

Clues to dating are gleaned from many different sources, the most important being manufacturers' catalogs, boxed toys which are known to be in unopened condition and of a determinable date, and dated photographs of children playing with toys. It is known, for example, that Britain's ARMY STAFF CAR, produced before and after World War II, had white tires prior to the war and black tires afterwards. A car marked "Made in Germany" would be pre-war, but one inscribed "Made in West Germany" is postwar. Either of the following sets of letters, "D.R.G.M.", Deutsches Reich Gebrauch Muster (a provisional patent mark) or "D.R.P.", Deutsches Reich Patent, is demonstrably pre-war. Toys which appear to represent pre-Great War vehicles may well have been made much later. Makers who were forced to turn their machinery to other purposes during hostilities, started up again using old models and continued to produce earlier designs, in some cases into the Thirties.

Dolls

Dolls have been made from terracotta, glazed stoneware, alabaster, rags, leather, wax and even gold. In the 18th century wooden dolls were popular. These "Flanders' babies", as they were known, had painted faces and moveable limbs held together with tiny wooden pins. Being fragile, few have survived. Around 1820 a sturdier ball and socket joint (still in wood) appeared.

New manufacturing techniques made it possible to produce low-priced poppets to feed the growing demand among lower paid workers and their offspring. Papier-mâché was the new wonder material. The unlikely combination of mashed paper, glue and plaster or leather scrapings produced an amazingly tough material: papier mâché dolls' heads were practically indestructible. The body would be fabric, wood, kid or earthenware. Today's relics often have scrappy bodies thanks as much to time's rough hands as those of their owners, the children. But the heads are nonetheless, very often in near mint condition.

If you come across a papier-mâché doll with painted eyes it may have been produced by America's earliest known papier-mâché doll maker, Ludwig Greiner; his work is believed to hark right back to 1845. Greiner made only heads, a gold or black label inside the head can clinch identification, the purchaser made a doll body to suit herself. A glass-eyed papier-mâché doll of similar date could well be German.

Often the young girl who owned the doll was given the task of making its clothes: what better way was there to inspire and instruct tomorrow's seamstress?

Paper dolls, even as recent as the brief and inglorious reign of Marilyn Monroe, are top of some collectors' shopping lists! The trick is to find them uncut—and also ungrubbied; easier said than done, apparently. Of course paper dolls go back a lot further than that: at least into the 19th century. There are comfortingly quick ways to date them, too. Look to the hair style. Hair curling into the neck was an 1840 vogue; short curls were an 1850 craze; the 1860s had a thing about *chignons*. Clearly most of the old paper dolls are behind glass in museums (beware the very good reproductions being occasionally sold as antiques).

The nearest you may get are paper dolls from the Thirties. Seven dollars can often buy you a celebrity or comic book paper doll, and Hicksville shops that have yet to launch themselves into modern slick selling have been known to yield dusty cutout dolls in original form and at the original price! The US firm of McLaughlin Brothers created dolls connected with newsy events and celebrities of the day. A paper

doll version of the 1869 betrothal of Lavinia Warren to P.T. Barnum's circus character Tom Thumb is known and keenly sought.

Especially desirable are "milliners' dolls". These feature the fantastic hair-does of the early 19th century, complete with bunches of ringlets piled high at the sides of the head and all faithfully reproduced in papier-mâché. The Germans liked to dip their papier-mâché dolls' heads into wax and then paint them; it gave all the appearance of a soft skin and the delicate bloom of a bonnie, bouncing baby. "Wax over composition" dolls, as these are known in the trade, are often sadly chipped or worn. All-wax dolls fared even worse and very few survive. The Plangonologist, technical name for the keen doll collector, is a stickler for detail and fusses over every aspect of dolls including teeth, complexion, eyes, hands, head, height.

It is said that some dolls were used by French couturiers to help spread the word about the latest Paris fashions. Such dolls are referred to as Parisiennes. Yet some collectors argue that only the larger, almost adult-sized dolls were fashion "mannequins". The smaller ones just served as a guide to the home dressmaker, they claim. The French excelled in producing elegant and beautifully dressed dolls.

Casimir Bru, a famous firm, set up shop in Paris in 1866. The Jumeau factory, established in 1842 became the most important and the biggest doll manufacturing company in the world. Jumeau specialized in *bébés* dolls that looked like small children, not babies. At the first international exhibition of 1851 Britain vied with France and Germany to produce the most attractive dolls. One reviewer commented: "The doll with the well-made body was indeed French, but the doll with the elegant head and the pretty face was certainly English".

A collection of doll's clothes made by a child in the 1860s.

In the 1830s doll makers began to use china for dolls' heads. And the first china heads, made by Meissen and Royal Copenhagen, were the best. Later dolls' heads were made of bisque (unglazed china) or Parian. (Bisque minus the coloring was known as Parian, since it resembled the white marble found on the island of Paros). As the 19th century progressed, dolls were to look less angelic and more like real human babies, wrinkles and all.

Bottle diggers sometimes pick up old dolls when they are searching through 19th century trash heaps. It appears that a lot of dolls from between 1880 and 1900 were made in Germany. The less energetic collector can hope to find old and interesting dolls in attics and boxrooms: the longer any one family lived in a particular house, the greater the chance of uncovering a worthwhile doll.

Dating of dolls in America is helped by a law of Congress of 1891, after which imported dolls had to be marked with the country they came from. Cloth bodied dolls can be examined for machine stitching, a facet which must post-date the invention of the sewing machine in 1850.

Anyone who comes across a hoard of early dolls' wigs will have a very valuable find indeed. The reason is that after 1918 dolls' hairstyles changed along with that of the fashionable belles of the day. Long hair was out and the short shingle and bob cut were in.Children promptly scalped their dolls to keep them looking up to date, and the dolls' wigs, with their flowing tresses, were instantly redundant and discarded.

There are doll hospitals, so even damaged dolls can be worthwhile,if the price is right: innumerable price guides are published, like M. Smith's 'Doll Values—Antique to Modern',or the 'Blue Book of Dolls & Values',(US) plus periodical literature even on rarified segments of this massively popular hobby, like the monthly Barbie Bulletin,available from 3824 W. Hazard, Santa Ana, California 92703.

Dolls' houses

It is one of those curious facts, often overlooked, that even the largest dolls' house is too small to accommodate even the smallest doll. Consequently collectors tend to treat dolls' houses independently of dolls. The first dolls' houses weren't houses at all. Nor were they meant to be played with. The Nuremberg kitchen, dating to the 17th century, was the forerunner of the dolls' house proper. It was simply a box meant to represent a room with a side or wall missing. The inside was a superb—and accurate—peepshow, showing a proper little period kitchen, complete with metal pots and pans, scrubbed pine furniture. Some sophisticated examples had working ovens. The experts believe that, far from being a toy, these set-pieces were used as domestic science models– to show young girls just what they were letting themselves in for as housewives. The Nuremberg kitchen, though initially a German idea, was quickly taken up by Dutch and other Continental makers. The English also had their one-room dolls' houses and filled them with careful carbon copies often no bigger than a thimble, of glasses, silverware and every other item of domestic furnishing.

Because every item was handmade in those days, only the wealthy could afford to expand the one-room diorama and add other rooms to form a makebelieve house. The earliest houses usually lack a staircase or hallways joining the rooms and the entrance, however. When dolls' houses began to appear in increasing numbers in stately homes it was evidently not as a plaything, but a showcase for magnificent adult miniatures.

As the 18th century drew to a close, and helped perhaps by the trend towards smaller homes with less room, the dolls' house lost its drawing room niche, but reappeared in the nursery as the toy we know today. Exteriors became more realistic; brightly colored brickwork was painted on and low-pitched roofs and chimneys were added. Interior staircases were included to make all the rooms accessible to each other. As architects abandoned the neo-classical influence that had produced some of our finest country houses, so the makers of dolls' houses abandoned their pint-sized copies to follow the latest housing trends: neo-Gothic towers and balconies were all the rage. One of the most remarkable and well-preserved survivors from the 19th century is the dolls' house that belonged to a certain Mrs Graham Montgomery. She acquired it in 1897, at the age of four, and kept it until she died in 1955. The house is seven feet long and five feet high, and modeled on the Elizabethan-style manor she lived in in Hampshire, England. The house has 18 rooms, including a Chinese room, night nursery and maid's room and a 1930s addition–a modern girl's room. The library boasts postage-stamp sized books and there is running water and an electric lighting system. This amazing relic of careful childhood and caring adulthood can now be seen in Edinburgh's Museum of Childhood in Scotland.

Banks and money boxes

The desire to save and store currency has been the inspiration for a variety of interesting containers now among the most cherished of collectables. There have been money boxes in the shape of pineapples, beehives, and an especially popular one looking like a mother hen sitting on her eggs. This should be a rich brown glaze over a pottery base. Cottage-shaped money boxes were once popular, and the best of these are decorated with trailing ivy, roses, honeysuckle and have little latticed windows, just like a real country cottage. But as

A cast-iron Jonah and the Whale money box.

you had to smash the cottage to get at the cash inside, there are few of these, or of any pottery boxes, still around.

Piggy banks are the best known money boxes; the theory is that this animal was chosen, partly because of its portly large-capacity shape, but also because the pig is a very economical beast: you can eat or use almost *every* part of it.

The collector differentiates between "still" and mechanical or novelty money boxes or banks. Cast iron mechanical money boxes from the last century were intended to amuse children and in so doing to encourage them to save; a spring or balance shoots the coin into the box.

The best early boxes came from Switzerland and Germany around the middle of the 19th century, but America was responsible for many of the most desirable money boxes, mass produced between c.1850 and 1910. One of the most famous American boxes is the Tammany Hall bank. These were linked with Will Tweed, an official who made the name of Tammany Hall, in New York, synonymous with corruption in public office. Look for a stout gent wearing a lounge suit sitting in an armchair. A coin placed in his left hand is instantly transferred to his top right hand pocket. Most Tammany Hall banks date from the last half of the 1870s. Often on the bottom you will see a mark which says "Pat'd June 8 1875", though this is not always a strict guide to age, and there have been many fakes.

Paddy and his pig is a favorite cast iron money box invented in 1882. Farmer Paddy is sitting, while his pig, nose in the air, is wedged between Paddy's legs. The penny is placed on the pig's nose and a spring makes his foreleg kick the coin into the farmer's mouth. Another cast iron treasure shows a dentist and his terrified patient. Press a button in the base of this toy and the dentist springs forward to slip a coin into his patient's gaping mouth. In the magician bank the magician stands on his iron pedestal in front of a miniature table. Place a coin on his table and press a lever at the side and the magician covers the coin with his top hat. When he removes the hat the coin has disappeared into the box. Curiously, the liveliest novelty banks are not always the most valuable.

Cast iron, though heavy and solidly constructed, is also brittle. An impatient little owner with the money lust would often "bounce" his box to extract the currency inside. And there were many accidental breakages. The Ferris wheel box made at the time of the Columbian Exposition of 1892 is one such fragile bank which suffered from its size and material and is now hard to find. Five years later came another collectors gem: a brightly colored iron Uncle Sam bank, made to mark the Philadelphia Centennial.

Patriotic banks are also high on the collectors' shopping list. Some show caricatures of hated enemy generals and leaders; others show famous heroes of the mother country or her allies.

A fairly new idea for money box collectors is "twinning". First you must discover what subjects were made in pairs; thus, we know that there was a money box in the shape of a boy leading a cow and also of a girl leading a cow. Male and female lions are also known. Collectors who prefer their money box collecting to be a "moving" experience should join the Mechanical Bank Collectors of America, c/o Charles Duff, 3803 Little St., Miami, Florida 33133.

Board games

The most sophisticated board game, chess, probably started in India and was later taken up by the Persians. The Indians called it *chaturanga*; the Persian corruption was *shatranj*. Masudi, an Arab author of the 10th century AD, wrote that chess had existed long before his time. Each culture added a little to the color and development of the game. The rook comes from the Persian *rukh*, meaning soldier; *shah mat*, Arabic for "the king is dead", gave us our checkmate. Around the 13th century the checkered two-color board was introduced. Castling was a western innovation, and the queen's rise to power is reckoned to be a 15th century European development: in eastern sets the king and queen both look like men.

Chess sets are known in wood, porcelain, horn, silver, crystal, glass, iron – there is even a grisly 19th century set in human bone. As the chess habit caught on in Georgian England simple wooden, pottery and pewter sets appeared, enabling even the lowliest households to play the game. Howard Staunton patented his famous design in 1849. Chess collectors prefer complete sets, but will occasionally settle for odd pieces of an unusual shape or theme — like the Russian propaganda set that features communists and capitalists: the workers are pawns bound in chains...

Games based on, but easier than, chess have been known for centuries. Draughts is connected with an Arabic game, Alquerque. It was invented in southern France in the 12th century and known there as "Dames". The Pilgrim Fathers took the game to America and re-christened it checkers. Look for handsomely turned ivory or bone and ebony draughtsmen and inlaid wooden games boards. Another chess-based game was "Asalto". This is also known as Officers and Sepoys (a Hindu or Mohammedan soldier in the British army in India); it caught on when the British Raj was at its height.

Many old board games are vividly colored, sometimes by hand, or printed and handsomely boxed. Collectors insist on being able to *play the game,* so the original rules should be included, as well as all the counters, dice, and so on.

John Jeffreys produced an interesting map board game in 1759; the theme was a journey through Europe. By throwing a die or spinning a totem the player was taken through European capitals and discovered interesting facts about the locations as well as how to spell place names. In a 1794 version of this game there are 117 towns and cities depicted on a fold-up board.

Ludo, based on an Indian game called Pachisi, started a vogue for Oriental games since its invention in 1896. Monopoly is likely to stay a popular game for as long as we live in houses, have landlords, prisons and cash. But the inspiration did not come from nowhere; there were similar games designed to hone the commercial instinct, such as Moneta and Game of Banking, and gambling games such as Good Going and Totopoly, for those who hoped to get rich quick without the effort. Collectable games date from about the mid 1800s to the

1920s, when radio and films took over as a lazy alternative to home-made entertainment.

Jigsaw puzzles

The first jigsaws appear to have been a 19th century map dealer's bright idea of what to do with excess stock: he pasted his maps on to wood and cut them up. Thus a new commodity, a toy, was created; one which had a U.S.P., a unique selling proposition, which could be profitably exploited. Parents could be persuaded that the new "dissecting puzzles" would actually educate their progeny.

John Spilsbury produced the first dissected map in 1762. In the 1760s he produced a series of at least 30 puzzle maps, and the map as a theme continued in popularity in the 1780s. The heavy-handed Victorians managed to turn a fun activity into an onerous duty, and introduced teaching puzzles which featured more text than picture, moralistic tales, religious themes, geography lessons, history tracts, maths tables, and so on. A history puzzle dated 1787 was attributed to C. Dilly and William Darton. It shows the heads of 32 English monarchs from William the Conqueror to George II and tells in explicit detail about their policies, lives and loves. A similar puzzle, by John Hewlett, was produced in the same year; John Wallace took a leaf out of both of their notebooks and brought out his own similar version a year later.

Inevitably, jigsaw puzzles were produced merely to entertain and not only to instruct. One of the most amusing of these shows a couple whose smiling faces, when viewed upside down, turn into snarling adversaries. The caption reads "Before and after marriage". Surprisingly, late 18th century jigsaw puzzles have often survived better than mid-Victorian ones, partly because the earlier boxes, of cedar and mahogany, afforded superior protection, and the printed pictures were mounted on hardwood, not flimsier wood or card. After around 1820 the top of the box would be decorated with a picture of the completed puzzle and mechanically sawn puzzles were introduced, with the pieces backed in strong thick paper to protect them while they went through the machine.

The complexity of the puzzle has little bearing on value to the collector. More important is originality of theme, quality of printing, completeness of pieces, original box in fine condition, etc. Especially desirable might be a double-sided puzzle dating to the second half of the 19th century. Curiously the two sides often had nothing in common, and might be something like a map on one side and a religious theme on the other. Great occasions are also important finds, such as a jigsaw commemorating the Great Exhibition of 1851, or a nostalgic creation, such as "the game of the star-spangled banner or immigrants to the United States" of 1835, a puzzle designed to wring sympathy from families whose kith and kin had crossed the Atlantic in search of fortune.

In the land of Disney

The idea for an animated mouse came to Walt Disney while he was traveling back on a train, from New York to Hollywood. He had just lost the rights to another cartoon creation, Oswald the Rabbit, to his financial backers. He remembered a tame field mouse he had trained while working in a studio in Kansas City. Disney dubbed the mouse creation Mortimer at first; but his wife thought that was too distinguished, so Disney renamed him Mickey and the legend was born. The first cartoon film featuring Mickey was inspired by Charles Lindbergh's historic solo flight from New York to Paris and was entitled "Plane Crazy". In 1928 Disney used the latest synchronized sound for "Steamboat Willie" which played to rapturous audiences in New York. The first use of Mickey Mouse outside the cinema was in 1930 when Disney was offered 300 dollars for the right to put a picture of Mickey on a school note pad. The Disney industry was an instant and overwhelming success and some of the items which have featured characters from the animal scrapbook are of a high quality as the owners of the copyright were reluctant to see their nationally known character decorated in tin-pot rubbish.

Today the collector looks for Mickey Mouse toothbrushes, watches, dolls, handkerchiefs, bracelets, children's cups and plates, cutlery, condiment sets, trains, annuals, comics, crayons, jigsaw puzzles and in the golden jubilee year of Mickey Mouse's creation, 1978, commemorative plaques and medals were also struck. The franchising of the mouse image enabled the studios to stay solvent through troubled times. Eventually a whole stable of animal characters appeared, including Pluto, Donald Duck, Goofy and more. Yet Mickey Mouse remains the best known and best loved of this Noah's Ark of characters. When war shut the cartoon factory the magic mouse was still in big demand. His grinning face, balloon-sized boots and black button nose appeared on many kinds of poster and emblems designed to help the war effort. Such items are worth their weight in gold-plated mouse-traps today. The Mickey Mouse image was also used to make children's gas masks more friendly and less frightening. And the price rises for Mickey Mouse collectables have been astonishing, given the throwaway price that they were once sold for. In 1934 a Mickey Mouse shooting gallery with target, gun and darts cost a mere 89 cents; a Mickey Mouse Ingersoll fob watch of 1933 was priced at 98 cents. In 1971 a Mickey Mouse watch was on sale in an Art Deco store and the owner was asking $38 for it; it eventually sold to Led Zeppelin's Jimmy Page who brought it for his lady. The American collector has access to an even wider range of Disney collectables, including the Mickey Mouse movie-jecktor and the first Mickey Mouse radio made in 1932 by Emerson — an object which can sell for some $500. A set of six Mickey Mouse figures made by William Britain, a name usually associated with model soldiers, went at auction early in 1980 for £750 ($1800). A tin-plate Mickey Mouse money box — you put the money on his tongue, pull his ear and watch him swallow the money — also made £750 at a British auction in 1980, and a Mickey Mouse barrel organ £150 ($350). At the other end of the scale, Mickey Mouse postcards go for two or three dollars.

3

For Bookworms And Browsers

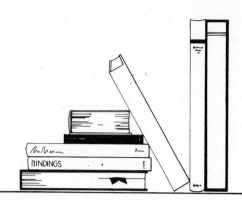

Books have become an international currency of such importance that it has been worth the while of some investment banks to buy up leading booksellers just to cut a few corners. A complete edition by Caxton or Wynkyn de Worde would buy a nice little retirement home in the country, yet an odd page from the hand of either printer could cost less than the price of redecorating the living room. There is something for every aspiring bibliophile - limitless variation within the most myopic category of collecting.

When buying an illustrated book make sure that all the pictures are present. Check at the front in the list of illustrations. Then turn to the back for there may be several pages of advertisements from the publisher's then current list or details of forthcoming books. All these advertising pages should be intact if the book is to be worth shelf space in your antiquarian library. The ads may list a group of books by the same author or on one topic, issued, often, in the same binding style. Find all those other volumes and you have a very valuable property.

The advertisements mentioned above can also provide a useful guide to the dating of first editions which most bibliophiles—dedicated book collectors—collect exclusively.

Sometimes a book will be dated in Roman numerals and it is worth learning how to read them: I = 1, V = 5, X = 10, L = 50, C = 100, D = 500 and M = 1000. Thus CCC = 300, XX = 20. But IX = 9 and XL = 40; the smaller figure, written first is deducted from the larger. If the first figure is the larger, the symbols are added together. For example, XI = 11. And there are, therefore, two ways of expressing certain numbers. The date 1934 could be written either MCMXXXIV or MDCCCCXXXIV.

Many booksellers issue catalogs listing stock with details of condition, price and size. A folio book indicates that pages have been folded over once from the original sheet; this usually means a large format, but it obviously depends how big the paper was to start. When the sheet has been folded twice, the name "quarto" is given—"4to" for short. Octavo, the size of most modern novels, is written "8vo".

Until you are familiar with the standards - and credentials - of a dealer you won't know how much faith to put in his descriptions of the wares he sells. A rough guide might go like this, however. "Mint" is meaningless; "fine" equals close on brand-new; "very good" is an average secondhand book; "good" means not much use; "fair" is on a par with poor; and "working" or "reading copy" is fit for the trash can.

A special kind of inscribed book is called an association copy. This is where an author has signed his own work or a famous owner has signed the book to mark it as his own. Good signatures can greatly enhance the value of a book.

Modern first editions are, by general consent, the books of British and American authors who have produced the bulk of their work in the past 50 years. The pantheon of collectable names includes C.S. Forester, P.G. Wodehouse, Virginia Woolf, Louis MacNeice, Alistair MacLean and E.M. Forster. Books like *A Passage to India* (already a classic and now fetching a handy sum for a good condition first) rub shoulders with such recently acclaimed works as *Watership Down*. (Finding a first of that is, by the way, about as tricky as trapping the rabbit hero of the book itself.)

You could limit yourself to a collection of only poetry, novels or drama. But given that many authors cross the boundaries it may well be more satisfying to choose a few favorite writers and aim to obtain a first of every one of their works. Accurately identifying firsts, and understanding the jargon of the bookseller and the bookbuyer takes a little study and practise. Some books helpfully state on the *verso*

A "penny dreadful" from 1871.

(reverse) of the title page "First Printing..." or "First Published...". Sometimes the book bears only one date but that is not the earliest date; it was merely changed each year with each fresh edition. The newer the book the easier it is to follow the lineage. As a general rule, if a book contains no information to the contrary, it probably is a first. Obviously if there is a mention of a second or third impression that volume is a reprint.

Another clue to status are the words "This edition...". Such books are described in trade catalogs as "1st Thus". These are not firsts. Sometimes a first impression will have subsequent *issues*. A second impression is as good as a 50th to the collector but the second issue can be quite acceptable. All it means is that a quantity of the first impression was held back to be issued later, possibly in a different binding. A bibliography must be consulted to uncover whether such was the case.

Dust covers or jackets are a vital part of post-1920 books, if one accompanied the volume when originally published. Not only is the dust wrapper a colorful addition to the work, but the artist who designed it may enjoy an equal status with the author. Besides, wrappers often reveal useful information about the writer and his previous publications. Dealers doubling as con-artists sometimes try to pass off genuine firsts clothed in jackets of a later date if the original is missing. Look for reviews of the book on the back of the dust cover. Only if the book had been previously published in, for example, the States, might there be reviews on the jacket of a British first, and *vice versa*. Also there may be mention of an author's later work.

Some firsts will fall into your lap, but others will take their toll in effort and cash expended. Many factors go towards establishing and modifying the price, desirability and availability. When Ian Fleming died there was a rush to buy James Bond firsts. Now only Fleming's first book, *Casino Royale,* is highly rated and fetches £450 ($1,000) if fine in the dust wrapper. Books that are acknowledged to be the author's best effort cost more. Leaders of lasting literary movements can command a high price, higher perhaps than writers whose work, although important, did not spawn a movement of lasting significance. *Waiting for Godot* (1952), for instance, a masterpiece by Beckett, founder of the theater of the absurd, can fetch several thousand for the first French limited edition of 59 copies, which was on sale in the theater on the first night! Yet *Look Back in Anger* (1957) by John Osborne, inspiration of the "Angry Young Men" of the Fifties, is typically £5 ($12) in mint condition in its dust wrapper (Faber).

RED JACKET,

A CHIEF OF THE INDIAN TRIBES, THE TUSCARORAS.

Frontispiece of an children's adventure book.

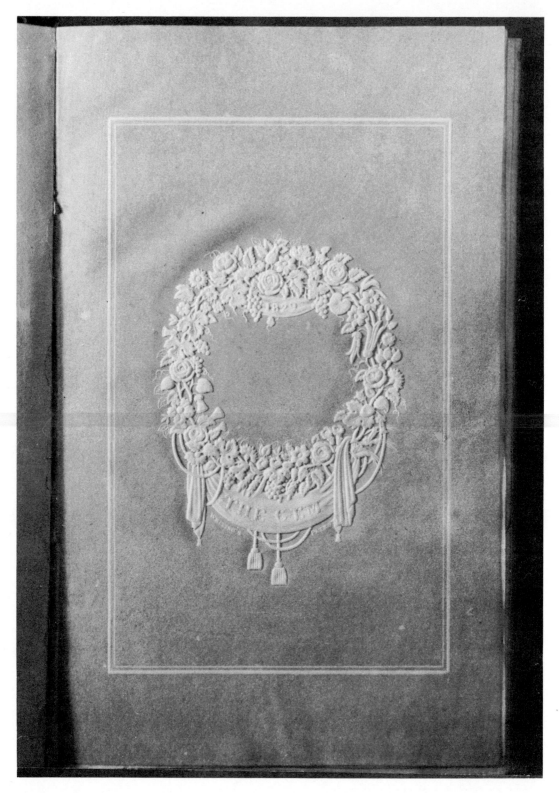

"The Gem" from 1829. A presentation plate in green, embossed in white.

Nostalgia may be a guiding factor at the check-out, rather than literary merit, as has been suggested is the case with the current uplift in prices of the work of the Beat Generation or the Liverpool Poets, Adrien Henry, Pete Brown, and Roger McGough. The latter's books and printed ephemera were part of the Beatles scene of the Sixties, an era which is enjoying nostalgic reappraisal at the moment. Concrete Poetry (possibly the most boring art form that never got off the ground) is also in for a price hike, according to the experts.

Ad hoc factors may also be at work on values. When *Alice in Wonderland* was first printed in 1865 Lewis Carroll objected so strongly to the poor printing that the issue was withdrawn and only about 20 copies are known to exist, one of which changed hands for £950 ($2,300) in early 1971 and that with a worn binding. Graham Greene hated the dust wrapper of *The Basement Room* and the book was recalled with only 100 being released. Subsequent issues command considerably less than the originally wrapped book.

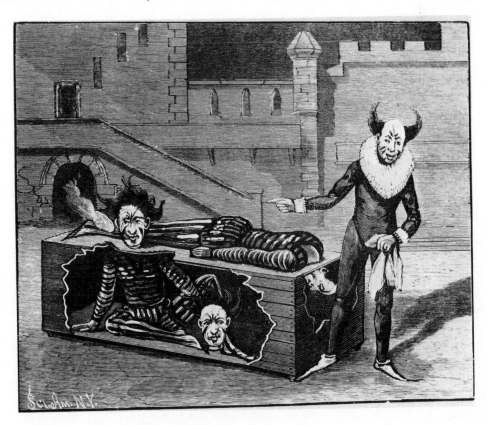

An illustration from a conjuring book.

Bookbinding, the outside story

The first bound books were made by monks. The first bindings were leather, wood or vellum, perhaps embellished with copper or silver mounting, set with mother of pearl, clad in rich brocade or even encrusted with gemstones. To keep a book's contents from prying eyes, and to prevent thieving fingers making off with individual pages, a book would often be fitted with clasps and a lock as well. There were many fads and fashions in binding, a knowledge of which can help you track down companion volumes at a glance and research the work of a particular binder. Sometimes a book would be emblazoned with a family crest or motto: and armorial style of decoration was popular from the 16th century. The Book of Common Prayer published by John Baskett in Oxford in 1716 had a characteristic "cottage" style binding which had become popular in the reign of Charles II and lasted for over 100 years. Recognize it by the broken pediment at the top and bottom of the gold inlaid central panel giving it a roof effect.

Tiny arabesques—little flourishes in the design—pepper the leather (usually morocco in the bindings but sometimes calf). Because this particular binding features a distinct S-shape it was possible to track down related volumes in other collections.

"Publishers' bindings" began in around 1740. Here the boards are stout card, not wood, and covered in marbled paper on the inside. The pages were folded over and left uncut at the edges, because the publishers' binding was temporary, meant merely to protect the book until the purchaser sent it to a binder, specifying his favorite style. Calf was the most popular material for private bindings, but the most valuable form of book today is that with the publishers' binding. Next in value is an early calf style. As a book became handled and worn so it would be rebound; the later the rebinding, the less valuable the book, is the general rule. The first book to be commercially bound in a full cloth binding was an early British annual, The Amulet of 1828.

At the beginning of the 19th century when graves and artefacts of the Etruscan peoples were discovered in northern Italy there was a vogue in bookbinding which imitated the motifs and colors of that long dead civilization. Books of the day appeared clad in terracotta color leather, often stained to suggest great age, and with helmets, urns and spears as their "classical" decoration. From the middle of the 19th century gift and prize books appeared which often featured panels of silk, tortoiseshell, wood and even porcelain. With the introduction of sophisticated machinery it was possible to die-stamp pictorial cloth

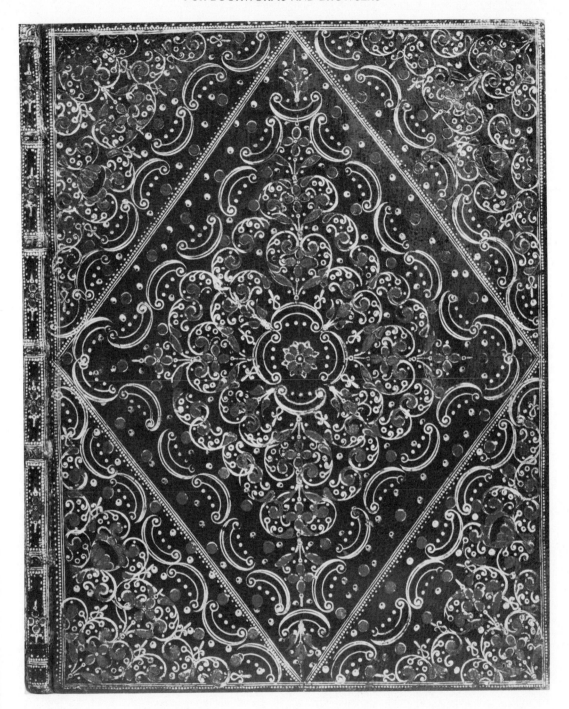

Binding by the Queen's binder for "Psyche, a tragedy", 1675.

covers in gold and silver. In 1918 an even cheaper means of brightening up books was introduced: the colorful dust-jacket. This was used to cover the often sombre leather or leather substitute binding, and as a sales gimmick it is with us to this day.

Book wrappers

The idea of books as packaged goods came late to the publishing industry. The wrapper was first used merely as protection for the book while in store and transit; eventually it became clear that there was scope for advertising forthcoming publications by printing on the back of the jacket. An attractive design and bold printing of the author's name, if he was famous, might also improve sales, and eventually an enticing résumé of the contents came to be included on the back or the fold over part of the jacket. Covers from the Art Deco years, the Twenties and Thirties, are easily recognizable from their angular shapes, hand done lettering and blocked in color. The work of a famous cover designer, like Edward Ardizzone, Richard Kennedy, or a selection of celebrated cartoonists who turned their hands to cover design, would make an interesting pictorial essay on the book jacket theme.

4

Charmed I'm Sure

Not all of the items included in this chapter are exclusively a female province: one of the most prolific collectors of hatpins was a man. Anyone, male or female, can appreciate the workmanship in *repoussé* silver in the top of a perfume bottle or the skill of the glass cutter. I collect pincushion ladies, those two-or-three-inch high porcelain figurines (top half only) which were once stitched to a little dress which doubled as a pincushion. The "hardware" is as collectable by a man as a woman, but the "soft wares", like lace, samplers, early clothing tend to be feminine preoccupations, perhaps as a throwback to a time when it was a common accomplishment for a woman to have "golden hands".

Hair jewelry

If a woman's hair was to be her crowning glory, then it needed jewels—or the appearance of gemstones and precious metal—truly to capture the look of regal beauty. Combs, clasps, and slides all qualify as hair jewelry. In the late 19th century even a small pin might be silver set or enameled; combs to keep back and sides neat could also be in silver or gold and glittering with real gems or semi-precious stones. Simpler combs came in mother-of-pearl, horn, tortoiseshell or ivory. To catch the eye the tops of these combs might be embellished with carved birds or butterflies. "Barrettes", special clasps or slides for holding strands of hair in place, were similarly decorated. Jeweled hair ribbons form a between-the-war years collector's favorite. Apparently it wasn't until the early 19th century that combs for grooming the hair came into use—a fact which apparently explains the popularity of scratching sticks with which a lady might surreptitiously relieve her itching scalp.

However, the main item that interests collectors in this field is the hatpin, produced in a formidable array of styles, lengths and metals from the last quarter of the 19th century up to the end of the Great War. Previously, an elaborate coiffure piled high had needed a quantity of hairpins which might be elaborate gold or silver ornaments or plain, depending on one's station in life. With the vogue for hats–especially the aptly named cartwheel hat—a substantial hatpin became a necessity, especially as even the most elaborate hats were worn atop a hair-do resembling nothing so much as the hanging gardens of Babylon. The first pins looked like metal skewers rather than elegant jewelry, but the best of the later versions have silver stems. The display end could be studded with a garnet, amethyst, cairngorm or topaz; moonstone, sea shell, jet, glass, ivory, ceramic and pearl tips are also known. Novelty hatpins include end-pieces in the shape of golf clubs or jolly hockey sticks. The cheaper end of the market includes musical instruments, animals and horseshoes. The most prized hatpins are those with swivel ends, so the glittering stone could be angled to catch the light, however the stem had been inserted in the hat or whichever side of the head it was worn. Valuable hatpins may conceal a vinaigrette, a smelling salts container; a screw-end hatpin may reveal a tiny powder puff with a concealed mirror. Crested porcelain ends by the firm of Goss are keenly sought, as are the regimental button-ended ones that became *de rigeur* during the Great War.

Hatpins up to 18 inches long are known, and although the device might have served a similar purpose to the sword-stick carried by many 19th century gentlemen, a razor sharp hatpin was often more of a liability than a defensive weapon in case of attack by an over-amorous unwanted suitor. In 1908 a newspaper reported: "A campaign against the murderous hatpin has been instituted by the newspapers of Berlin, in view of the series of accidents which have already occured in the busy period of Christmas shopping. Numbers of more or less serious injuries have been caused by these dangerous implements protruding from the huge hats of fashionable ladies. Last Sunday a lady was permanently blinded in one eye when taking part in a rush at a 'bargain sale' ".

A collection of hatpins.

In November, 1980, Phillips, the London auction house, mounted their first exhibition devoted entirely to hatpins. The more than 2,000 hatpins coming under the hammer were the collection of, believe it or not, a man: 38-year-old Clive Marchant, a hatpinologist of 21 years' standing. Apparently he was given some 300 pins and the fad stuck; within a year he had doubled his stock and was well on his way. When he exhibited his hatpins at an antiques fair in the Seventies, the official description read: "There are hatpins of filigree work, of piqué, simulated piqué, brilliant mosaic, precious and semi-precious metals in both classical and Art Nouveau styles, souvenirs of...Ireland, birds modeled in glass, a selection in ivory... Another group features famous regimental badges, perhaps made by soldiers in the Boer War and Great War."

A hatpin collection looks best if displayed in an original hatpin holder. There are two main kinds: one, often of silver, looks like a miniature umbrella stand with a pincushion for a base; the other often in porcelain, resembles a candlestick with a pierced pepper-pot top.

61

Fans

The very earliest form of fan was made not to cool the user but to swat flies. Fly fans came from the East to the West in 1307, but it took the gallant eye of Henry VIII of England to see the sartorial possibilities of the fan. Under his tutelage every courtier owned at least two fans: one long one to use as a parasol while out walking, and a short one for dress purposes. Queen Elizabeth I popularized the folding fan. The necessity was for a leaf as light as silk, for comfort, but as strong as hide to withstand the constant folding; it was found in the skin of an unborn kid. Specially dressed and treated, it had a grain so fine it could only be seen when held to the light. Today's collector covets these "chicken skin" fans, as they're known.

In the 18th century a bizarre "fan language" developed. It was a kind of social semaphore. According to one perceptive observer "A Spanish lady with her fan might shame the tactics of a troop of horses. Now she unfolds it with a slow pomp, and the conscious elegance of the bird of Juno; now she flutters it with all the languor of a listless beauty, now with all the liveliness of a vivacious one. Women are armed with fans as men with swords and sometimes do more executions with them."

An amusing fan: Painted panels in the shape of lily leaves, mother-of-pearl sticks.

An academy sprang up in London to teach the debs of the day "fan talk". Books on the topic appeared explaining the moves: twirling the fan in the left hand meant "we are being watched". Touching the tip of the fan with the finger was a way of saying "I wish to speak to you". Foppish men, too, became adept at twirling a fan. It was said that there were three sexes: men, women and Herveys. Lord Hervey, who always carried a fan, became known as Lord Fanny...

There are several kinds of fan; the most common, in the West, being the *éventail* or folding fan. This consists of a number of sticks or blades, the skeleton or framework, and the leaf. The leaf could be vellum, textile, silk, lace, or parchment cut as a segment of a circle. Another type of collapsible fan is the *brisé* fan. This is made entirely of blades, joined together by elaborately threaded ribbons. *Brisé* fans were often made of ingeniously fretted ivory blades: "frozen lace" is one historian's apt description of the look of a carved ivory *brisé* fan. Blades were also made of bone, amber, horn, feather, lacquered woods and tortoiseshell. The *brisé* fan enjoyed a vogue from the 1680s and became the rage in the 18th century thanks to the patronage of Madame de Pompadour who was fascinated by ivory.

Unusual fans include the telescopic variety designed to slip into the purse, the dagger fan with a deadly blade concealed in the handle; the quizzing fan of c.1735 had spy holes cut into the sticks to enable a hypocritical lady to watch risqué plays without jeopardizing her reputation. The flirtatious domino fan had cut-out eyeholes; painted to look like velvet or lace, it was used as a mask. Trade fans bearing printed slogans, or announcements of events are among the cheaper varieties. Souvenir fans decorated with signed engravings of important people and famous places are well worth buying when you see them.

Scent containers and perfume bottles

In Medieval times, long before bottles of perfume became popular, a special pan—the perfume pan—was used to carry the fragrance of burning herbs and spices from room to room: keeping a noble house smelling sweetly was the task of the Official Perfumer. As an alternative to the pan, liquid essences were poured into tiny silver trays with shallow sides. The top was pierced so the aroma could escape and deodorize a room. Priests and doctors especially needed to ward off evil fumes when they went among the sick. A dried orange, drenched in essences and studded with cloves, would be kept in a box or locket known as a pomander.

The name *pomander* is a corruption of the French *pomme d'ambre* or amber apple, the amber being ambergris, a waxy, sweet-smelling extract from the intestines of the sperm whale. To make the "apple" even more potent, lavender, nutmeg, musk, mace and cloves in rose water were added. Pomanders made of jeweled, beaten gold or intricately worked silver, no bigger than an inch across, were made to dangle from a chain round a pretty wrist or neck.

Around 1530 the pouncet-box appeared. This was a shallow case with a domed and perforated lid, also of precious metal, designed to hold a sponge drenched in spiced vinegar. Henry VIII, along with his nobles and the fashionable gentry, had pouncet-boxes built into the tops of their ebony staves. Sniffing one's pouncet-box became an elegant, almost effeminate, art and one of the social graces of the day. Shakespeare in King Henry IV captures the mood beautifully:
"He was perfumed like a milliner;
And betwixt his finger and his thumb he held
A pouncet-box, which ever and anon
He gave his nose, and took't away again."

The golden age of the perfume bottle was the 18th century. A gentleman who wanted to impress his lady-love would send her perfume as a gift in a bottle made of fish skin; such presents were known as *Galanteriewaren*.

Porcelain was another favorite material for a love token. Chelsea smelling bottles often depicted a human figure or animal exquisitely molded in the hard paste. The stopper might be disguised as a bouquet of tiny porcelain flowers or perched birds in later examples. A clue to the earliest Chelsea ware is a deep base; this was used to hold patches, tiny black shapes used by fashionable women to conceal a skin blemish.

Wedgwood produced perfume bottles decorated with tiny cameo portraits of classical figures, milky white against a darker matt clay background. The true perfume bottle is usually small, because of the cost of the essence, airtight and opaque; sunlight is harmful to scent. The bottle would be carried in a purse, tucked in a glove pocket or kept hanging from the wrist or a heavy chain or chatelaine. Larger bottles are probably meant for the dressing table or bathroom shelf. Early glass perfume bottles are today's most cherished possessions of collectors who like to follow their noses and don't have a fortune to spend. Clear, cut glass perfume bottles can be roughly dated according to their decoration. Up to 1790 only shallow cuts were possible; deep cutting came in later, especially elaborate work being produced in Regency times, approximately 1800 - 1830. At the end of the 18th century England's Bristol was producing opaque white, deep blue, amethyst and green glass. Sometimes the bottles were embellished with gold and silver. Though a hallmark will reveal the date of manufacture, if the weight of metal was too low it may not have merited the official stamp yet may still be precious metal. From the late 19th century up to World War II, leading French parfumiers commissioned top glass artists to design bottles for their exclusive perfumes, among them Gallé, Lalique and Daum Frères.

Chatelaines

It is only fairly recently that men have managed to overcome the evident stigma they feel is attached to making sensible provision for carrying about all the essentials that go with modern living, like keys, banknotes and coinage, pocket-knives, nail files, all of which, in the case of a woman, together with a whole artist's palette of facial confectionary, normally fits snugly inside a handbag. Now men who wear denims are happy to carry a clasp, attached to their belt or belt-loop, to hold keys; and there is also a rather faltering vogue for flat, neat leather satchels to wear over the shoulder or clutched in hand as a kind of male handbag substitute. It was the idea of having all one's portable accessories conveniently to hand, in the absence of pockets, that prompted the development of the chatelaine in the 18th century. Europe's wealthy carried an astonishing variety of hardware around with them and it was convenient to have these hanging by chains from a belt or sash around the waist.

A single chatelaine might boast as many as ten items hanging from rings or chains, but the average is five items. The paraphernalia included seals, watches, watch keys (to wind the watches), scissors, bodkins, button hooks, vinaigrettes, needle cases, pencils, *étuis* (small cases for holding valuables), charms, rulers, thimbles, cutlery, compasses—as well as door keys. Men's chatelaines were longer than women's; sometimes a man would wear two chatelaines, one on either thigh to conceal the openings in the flap of his breeches, the earliest form of fly. Matthew Boulton of Birmingham produced severe-looking chatelaines of cut steel especially for men.

The earliest chatelaines (now coveted as objects of vertu and priced accordingly) are highly ornate, often in precious or semi-precious stone and set in gold or silver-gilt or pinchbeck, an alloy of copper and zinc, or marcasite. The often triangular clasp from which the chains were suspended, the chatelette, is a collectable in its own right. A complete chatelaine, designed as a piece, is a rarity.

The more elaborate creations died out by around 1800, but silver chatelaines continued into the late 19th century. The chatelaine, in abbreviated form, continued right up to World War I, but by then was designed to hold little more than a fob seal. Chatelaine seals are collectable by themselves. Early all-gold or silver seals display intaglio cut coats of arms. Swivel-mounted seals were cut on two or more faces with a different emblem or amusing design; each face could be turned to meet the mood of the user or the importance of the correspondence. Seals, set in gold, pinchbeck or gilded metal, were cut into agate, bloodstone, onyx, cornelian, topaz or sapphire. A late craze for tiny silver envelopes meant to hold postage stamps lasted from around 1880 to 1910.

Lace

The Elizabethans had their heads bent almost double with lace neck ruffs made of lace perhaps a yard deep and 25 yards long. Henry III of France was buried in bolts of frothy, spidery lace. Dead or alive, you needed to be rich to own lace–but not any more. Lace, to frame under glass and against a background of deep blue silk or tissue, or to incorporate into a modern outfit, is easy to find at rummage sales and clothing auctions. Lace is virtually impossible to fake; the main problem is distinguishing between genuinely hand made and machine made lace (which could in any case have been made over 100 years ago).

Any flimsy, filmy material may be called lace. The earliest *lacis* (darned net) may feature simple geometric patterns or figures in Tudor costume, such as equestrian damsels riding side saddle. Though *lacis* was revived in the last century, you should take care that your find is really as old as it looks from the characters. In cut-work, a development that followed the earliest darning experiments, the needlewoman worked on a linen base, drawing out the threads; eventually the openings became the prominent feature and the background got lost in the airy pattern. The material was kept firm by whipping over the threads with a strong buttonhole stitch. True antique lace is usually either "needlepoint" lace or bobbin, otherwise known as "pillow" lace.

Both types of lace were made from scratch—that is, there was no net

Mid-18th century French bobbin lace

background for a foundation, no embroidery or drawing together of threads. Needlepoint or needle-made lace was made by sewing and sewing a design with looped buttonhole stitches. The piece took shape from a single thread carried on a needle. In pillow lace many strands were used. A pricked-out pattern was tacked to a firm pillow, and pins inserted to mark out the pattern. The lace thread, carried on a bone or wooden bobbin, was looped around each pin; a separate bobbin was used for each thread and there may have been a couple of hundred bobbins used for just one piece of lace. The art of twisting and manipulating the threads to create the pattern led to the many varieties of lace, which in themselves form a long and fascinating study.

As a general rule, the finer the thread the older the lace. Knowledge of typical fashions of the period can also help you date a lace oddment: 17th and 18th century pieces often have scalloped edges, the earlier they are the deeper the scallops. A typical 17th century design from the Netherlands was the "potten kamp" or flower-in-a-pot, a design that frequently crops up on old Dutch tiles. A prize lace is Venetian *gros point*. The edges of petals and flowers appear in delicate filigree worked lace, or are heavily stitched to give a striking three-dimensional effect. Berthas or shoulder flounces are typicaly mid-Victorian; they were meant to frame a daringly low-cut neck-line.

Nineteenth century ladies' handkerchiefs, usually of lawn, cambric or fine white linen, were often edged in lace, providing a low-price selection of study pieces for the beginner collector. This idea of a handkerchief bordered in lace (often the smaller the handkerchief the wider the border) was a 19th century fad. The size of a lace handkerchief is a giveaway to age, in many cases. It was in 1840, when fans dropped from favor, that large handkerchiefs—up to 25 inches square—came in. Ten years on, handkerchiefs were only 19 inches wide and by 1870 they had shrunk still further. By 1930, a handkerchief was barely big enough to blow a nose on.

To be able to tell mechanical from handmade lace, invest in a powerful magnifying glass. Handmade lace was silk, flax or even human hair (*point tresse*); machine made lace was always cotton or synthetic fibre. Recurring errors point to a machine at work, while in handmade garments you can sometimes see the joins in a single flaxen thread appearing every 20 inches or so. Apparently in hand spinning continuous threads were hard to make. Mechanically made lace is quick to unravel, whereas needlepoint handmade lace is a devil of a job to unpick. Try rolling up lace, for another swift guide to vintage. The handmade variety rolls softly and is smooth to the touch; machine lace is more rigid.

Samplers

Long before the days of ready-to-wear clothing, needlework was a common accomplishment of the cultured woman, who might spend months painstakingly sewing with silk, gold and silver threads. Much as a woman today collects knitting patterns, so yesterday's woman liked to collect favorite sewing tricks, new designs, and so on. The idea of a sampler, a needleworker's "practise pad", came into being from the 15th century. The first samplers were just scraps of handwoven linen, but gradually a more sophisticated form developed and patterns were handed down through families. From about 1640 to 1750, the most popular designs included flowers like honeysuckle, lilies, pansies and more exotic varieties like Arabian roses and Persian pinks; strawberries and acorns were common patterns; so, too, were creatures like caterpillars, lions, unicorns, leopards, stags and crickets.

The most curious design to be seen, however, is the little hobgoblin which appeared about the time of the Restoration. These little "boxers", as they were known, were usually embroidered in silk on white linen; each carries a goblet in his outstretched hand, and each pair of hobgoblins is separated by a needlework tree. No one knows quite what they represented, although theories have been put forward. Some believe they show the jester with some kind of trick in his hand . Or the figure may represent the gambler's devil, and the vessel is his cup of dice.

The 17th century fashion for lace-trimmed ruffs and accessories encouraged production of white samplers featuring cut-work and lace stitches, together with drawn-thread work. But as the fashion declined, towards the end of the century, so samplers began to change from being a genuine practical guide for the needleworker to become a kind of tour de force—a permanent record of superlative skill and showing the full repertoire of an individual. The sampler maker might also add her name and date and perhaps also a proverb or some other edifying text. Curiously, but fortunately, these early samplers have often outlived those that were made in later years, for moths shun linen but thrive on the worsted or "Tammy-cloth" backing used for samplers till about 1825.

The samplers that then started to be produced in schools, the work of of reluctant and hard-pressed schoolgirls, show that the pleasant pastime had turned into a nervewracking chore. A 10-year-old pupil at a charity school gave vent to her own tedium, in thread, with the following couplet: "This I have done, I thank my God,/Without correction of the rod". Tombs, urns and cherubs were all characteristic motifs of 18th century: evidently the more morose the design, the later in that century it was worked. Nineteenth century children incorporated letters of the alphabet into their samplers and it is believed that these became a kind of reading primer. In the 1850s the equivalent, for samplers, of painting by numbers made its appearance with pre-printed patterns and special wool (Berlin) to use. These later examples lack the freshness and spontaneity of the earlier era.

Because samplers sometimes carried both the date and age of the girl

Late 17th century needlework picture of the finding of Moses.

who had produced it, you sometimes find that these have been unpicked: the vain woman of later years was not keen to have her true age telegraphed to the world!

Sewing machines

Many of the elements of the successful sewing machine were in existence well before it was possible to produce a working model. Charles Weisenthal contributed, in 1755, an embroidery needle which had the eye at the pointed end; at the end of the century British cabinet-maker Thomas Saint patented a machine for "stitching, quilting or sewing"; Saint had mastered many of the mechanical ingredients necessary, on paper at least: but it is not known whether he ever fulfilled his patent, which specified an overhanging arm, carrying the needle, a continuous supply of thread and a horizontal cloth table or plate—just as on a modern machine. In 1830, Thimmonier, a French tailor, created a chain-stitching machine that used a barbed needle: it needed an extraordinarily steady hand to maintain a regular size stitch. Other inventors tried to imitate the movements of the human hand in iron and steel, and their quaint attempts can sometimes be seen engraved in early scientific publications.

Three American inventors, Walter Hunt, Elias Howe Jnr., and Allen Wilson, independently helped iron out the wrinkles in the "iron seamstress". But it was Singer who patented the first practical domestic sewing machine. Isaac M. Singer, skilled cabinet-maker, mechanic and marketing genius, had the unique American flair for salesmanship. To help push his machines he demonstrated them to social groups and church gatherings; he used gorgeous girls as demonstrators in sumptuous showrooms; he showed his sewing machines at the circus. And most effective of all, in 1856 Singer introduced payment by instalments. In 1850, Singer was producing 850 machines a year; by 1876 the Singer Manufacturing Company was churning out a quarter of a million models annually.

But it had not been an altogether easy fight. Seamstresses had worked at pitiful rates to gain a crust and the girls were afraid that even their low wage was at risk from the new invention. In 1854 *Household Words*, a magazine, posed the question: "Will the iron seamstress drive the seamstress of (not much) flesh and blood to more remunerative employment?" At the time a shirt took 14 hours to make by hand, but a machinist could run one up in under an hour and a half. Inevitably, progress could not be halted.

As far as collectors are concerned, a Singer even 100 years old may be worth little—whatever a store offers as a trade-in on a new machine. Only a few of the very early Singers are prized, among them models carrying the patent date 1851. Look, too, to the base of the machine for its serial numbers: numbers 1-12,000 were large semi-industrial type machines, not very attractive but rare. Much more pleasing is the Family or Turtleback machine made between 1858 and 1861. The traverse Shuttle Letter A is another interesting Singer oddity. Made between 1859 and 1865, its distinctive feature is the shuttle which moves from left to right, rather than backwards and forwards; it also has an eye-catching base in the shape of a fiddle, the square shape of the arm distinguishing it from a similar fiddle-based machine, the New Family, that went on sale from 1865. The latter boasts more flowing lines and a smooth bend in the elbow joint of its arm.

Singer also made de luxe versions, finely finished cabinets handsomely inlaid with mother of pearl. But the most popular machines with collectors who do not have their own warehouses are the diminutive variety: generally speaking, the smaller a sewing machine the more it is worth. The Moldacot Pocket Sewing Machine, made in the UK from 1886 and clipped to the table top was only hand high. Favorite makes include the Willcox and Gibbs single thread chain stitch machine. The head of this model forms the letters G. Willcox and Gibbs S.M. Co. may be painted in gold on the arm. Unusually shaped machines also carry a price premium, especially the Dolphin, the arm of which looks like a curving back of a sea beast, and the Cherub, made by the same firm, which incorporates a magnificently cast pair of cherubim. The treadle-powered Wheeler and Wilson sewing machine has an interesting throw-back to an earlier fashion in the casting of the treadle: there is a pair of cast iron footprints to help you place your feet correctly. However, the shape of the sole is long and pointed, to match the pinched shoes that were high fashion in the 1870s.

Quilts and coverlets

Quilting is a traditional craft that dates back to the Middle Ages. Quilted garments were found to be warm and light. In the 17th century quilted breeches, quilted doublets, waistcoats and even quilted petticoats were worn in Britain. Quilting can be tough, too, and quilted garments were used to deflect blunt missiles on the battlefield, or a quilted lining was worn under metal armor.

The bed quilt has a flock, combed cotton or down lining inserted between usually two layers of material, the lining being held in place with stitches or tying. Quilts, always made to last, were handed down from mother to daughter and made up using bits of cloth that had themselves been saved up over the years and were possibly already "antique". By one method patches were cut and mounted on calico or camlet, with turnings which were folded under and hemmed down. Unbleached calico and chintz were also turned into quilts, the calico being decorated with embroidery first. The "crazy quilt", made up of odd-shaped scraps (pieced patchwork) is common to both the States and Europe. But the idea of appliqué patchwork in quilts has always had a stronger hold in the United States.

From Holland and England the settlers took their needlework skills to America where the craft flourished and popular patterns earned themselves bizarre nicknames, like Broken Plaid, Single and Hanging

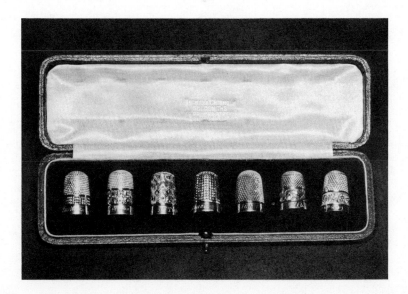

Silver thimbles engraved with the names of the lost boys
from J. M. Barrie's Peter Pan.

Diamond, Turkey Tracks, Death's Black Darts and Geometric Snowball. Lines of elaborate stitching added swirling shell shapes and scrolls to the quilt; Ocean Wave, Lover's Knot and Twisted Rope all describe traditional stitched patterns. In the US quilting flourished in a uniquely chummy way; the "quilting bee" was a party held usually before hay-making. The star was a girl about to get married. Her guests, neighbors and friends, gathered in the girl's home early in the morning around the quilting frame. Sewing materials were there in abundance. The object of the party was to create, on the spot, a handsome wedding gift for the couple - and to complete it before the sun set.

The front panel of a 19th century Chinese silk embroidered skirt.

5

Mainly For The Male

Art and artifacts of the American Indian

It used to be possible to pick up lowly American Indian relics like a pair of beaded moccasins for mere coinage; now you could pay less for a pair of Gucci boots! The least exciting US house sale would yield pocketfuls of old arrowheads, pottery, dolls; rugs could almost be whipped out of the tepee, from under the feet of its owner. Now little remains, outside of museums, that is earlier than the 1930s. Curiously, however, there may be some good hunting to be done in the UK, where there has long been a devoted coterie of cowboy and Indian fanatics. Not that they are ignorant of the true worth of their possessions, but since American museums have largely ceased their policy of swopping with private clients, it may yet be possible to make useful exchanges with UK collectors without a penny changing hands.

The Bible of the British collector is a quarterly known as The Brand Book, put out by the English Westerners' Society. Issues have appeared featuring the development of the Colt and an illustrated history of the headgear of the Plains Indian. Also, there is a specialist dealer in Wild West memorabilia with a foot in both camps: Wild West Imports are at 6660 Maryland Drive, Los Angeles, California 90048 and at 25 Middle Road,

A selection of Indian jewelry.

Harrow on the Hill, Middlesex, England. The last time I spoke with their Doris Wilson she was handling early US copper and silver coinage which had been prettily fretted away from its circular frame and made up into necklets (let the purists shriek; as far as Wild West is concerned, you take what you can get), and also Buffalo Bill period medallions.

A keen collector explained that a lot of goodies came to Britain through people who worked for the Hudson's Bay Company. Their souvenirs included coveted bead and porcupine quill work, a rather hazardous art apparently, and unique to the American Indian. The dyed quills were soaked, then the weaver would sit with a bunch of quills in her mouth - a bit dangerous, as they are barbed! - and she'd take them out one at a time, using her nails to flatten them. Porcupine quill work pre-dates bead decoration. Later, as beads became more easily available, quill work ceased. Dating clues lie in the type of beads used. The first, trade, beads were actually used as currency. The earliest varieties were porcelain colored white and blue, and they came from Italy in the early 1800s. Together with quills—dyed, flattened and ingeniously woven—they were incorporated into beautifully patterned work. Later beads were gaudier; seed beads of 1840 and the 1850s came in many colors with bright red a common favorite. Earlier examples may have a white core and are a more subtle, coral hue. Beads used to be sewn with sinew, another giveaway guide to authenticity and an early date. On the finest work, no stitches show at the back of the sewn pieces. Large beads, by the way, most probably indicate a date not later than 1870. Beadwork resembling French crewelwork could be from the Alonquin tribes in the Great Lakes who came into contact with the French settlers there.

The Indians loved decoration and they made artistic use of whatever pretty materials came to hand: French brass beads, bone and shell, and much else besides. One breastplate in the collection of a friend features twin rows of bone rollers. The rollers were almost certainly made by white men and sold to the Indians. Original Indian-made rollers would have been manufactured out of the center of the conch shell. Sometimes their hair was drawn through these tubes, when they are known as "hair-locks" or "hair-pipes". My friend's breast-plate example could be Sioux, but is more probably of Cheyenne parentage.

Collectors in this tricky market should stay with one tribe. Easier said than done, maybe, until you know how to recognize the handiwork of each. The Plains Indians—the mounted warriors who featured most often in those rip-roaring cinematic yarns in which the truth became as flexible as celluloid enjoyed a brief (c.1830-90) but vivid flowering of their culture. They are famed for their beadwork, embroidery and leather painting. The Navajo are known for their superb rugs: to know the characteristic patterns and colors is to be able to date the rugs. Soft, vegetable dyed rugs, in striped patterns, are likely to be pre-1800; squares and shapes appear from the turn of the 19th century to about 1875. Factory dyes and commercially produced wool point to the growing influence of white settlers in the fin de siècle period. There was also a tendency to tone down the palette, in favor of grays, browns and white. By the Deco years brightness had returned and it is possible to confuse work of this period with genuine early stuff–so beware.

American Indian jewelry is especially well collected. When a tribe went on the warpath the braves would bedeck themselves with a variety of necklaces, bracelets, rings and amulets, usually in solid silver and encrusted with turquoise. Only seven years ago I was offered, for around $500 (£250 then), a magnificent silver and turquoise "squash blossom" war necklace with *najahe* set with 15 slabs of turquoise. From about 1795 the Navajo Indians wore jewelry into battle and one of their favorite motifs was the *najahe*, an inverted horseshoe shape derived from the Phoenicians of Tyre of antiquity. Apparently the design passed to the Moors and came to the Americas courtesy of the Spanish conquerors. The Navajos believed the *najahe* would ward off the evil eye.

Other favorite battle-dress trinkets were the *ketoh* or wrist guard— it stopped a bowstring slashing into the wrist when the arrow was released—and chunky silver belts. The latter were often made up with *conchas,* shell-like ornaments strung on leather thongs. Collectors who buy conchas could be making an investment similar to that originally intended by the Navajo and Zuni tribes who went in for such belts in the 19th century: whenever an Indian found himself tight for cash, he'd slip off a concha and sell it. As virtually all the silver of the Indians in the south-western states was obtained from Mexican coinage, this was a strikingly apt way of re-realizing capital.

Take care to distinguish between "pawn" and "trade" jewelry pieces. Trade describes jewelry the Indians made expressly to sell; look for giveaway signs like the flatness of the turquoise cabochon, the thinness of the silver and cursory attention to detail. Pawn pieces the Indian intended to keep—if he didn't fall on hard times. The very earliest items were merely decorated by filing, engraving or simple incision. Die-stamping followed and repoussage (embossing) is later still. Although the turquoise adds interest to the purely silver pieces it is a pointer to a later date, probably no earlier than 1880 and possibly as late as the early years of our own century.

Fake plastic turquoise is a must to avoid, as are the make-believe, but very convincing, studio props put out by Metro Goldwyn Mayer; these found their way on to the market, in all innocence, in the late Sixties. Collectors who don't have their own Last Chance Saloon to furnish or the capital, may prefer to buy modern handmade Indian jewelry, or settle for the most modest of the old artifacts, the baskets. To learn more about Indian art and craft read *200 Years of North American Indian Art* by Norman Feder; artist George Catlin's *Manners, Customs, and Conditions of the North American Indians; Indian Art of the United States,* published by the Museum of Modern Art, New York; and *Indian and Eskimo Artifacts of North America* by Charles Miles.

Dolls in buckskin clothes made by the Kilkitat Indians in the 19th century.

Cameras, conspicuous and candid

For some reason, collectable cameras seem to have migrated to Britain over the years. The world's keen collectors and dealers, particularly the Germans, visit the UK regularly to replenish their stocks of home-manufactured cameras. One of the sad but unsurprising aspects of being overrun in war is that the conquerors take home souvenirs, cameras among them. The Japanese are similarly taken with sophisticated metal cameras like the Leica, but are unmoved by the more romantic wooden cameras. Americans, on the contrary, are, like their collecting cousins in the UK, keen buyers of wooden cameras, especially tropical ones. Do collectors use their old cameras? Not often. But they do like the parts to work or appear to work, so they can focus, and release the shutter — even if the speed is wildly out.

Early Leicas are among the cream of collectable cameras. The Leica 1, with fixed lens, the world's first miniature camera, appeared back in 1925 and more than 100 models followed. You won't have to pay much over £50 ($125) for a rough condition Leica 111a (1935-1938), over £100 ($250) for a fine one, a worthy, sturdy and very useable camera. The lenses are "slower" than many modern cameras—you need longer exposures in poor light, which may limit hand-held shooting indoors and on wintry days. And the wind-on mechanism, with early Leicas, is operated by twirling a knurled knob, not the flick-of-the-wrist lever-wind of today's cameras. But the results can be superb—and you have made a shrewd investment. Rather more recherché Leicas include the c.1959 German army issue camera. Early Leicas tend to be all black, later ones black and silver alloy; the green army model complete with matching olive case and telephoto lens, as well as standard lens—was made in c.1959 by the famed Wetzlar factory. Only a handful of this adapted M1 model are believed to have been issued.

Leicas bearing the Nazi swastika are at a premium and will make quite a fancy price in the saleroom. Another Third Reich collectable is the Robot, a 35mm camera incorporating the first mass produced automatic film advance. A spring wound gadget attached to the top plate enabled 15 to 20 shots to be taken in quick succession. A nice condition specimen can make upward of £100 ($250).

For certain professionals, the Press especially, it is often convenient to have more than the standard 36-exposures to a roll of film. In 1934 Leica introduced its 250 model with massive round chambers at each end containing 33ft of film and offering 250 exposures. Evidently reporters found them a bit cumbersome, but the 250 found favor with beach photographers in the Thirties.

Another Leica model geared to the professional was the MP (1956). This had a built-in Leicavit attachment—a rapid winding device—incorporated into the base. You can pick up a Leicavit, by itself, as an accessory, for £80 to £90 (about $200) in a British saleroom.

John Jenkins, director of Vintage Cameras of London, cites the Leica 111g (1957), at around £400 ($1,000), as an up-and-coming collector's camera because it was the last of the screw lens models. Inevitably, as one link in a collecting chain slips out of reach, pricewise, of the aficionado, so the "next best thing" becomes desirable, and sure enough, the early bayonet mount lens Leicas are now being more closely scrutinized in the market place. The neatest, cheap guide to Leicas and Rolleiflex are the Focal Press booklets. Morgan Taylor, a Leica buff with a magnificent collection, offers a hospital service for ailing Leicas from his home at "Crouchlands", Whiteman's Green, Cuckfield, Sussex, England.

Rolleiflex, the original twin-lens reflex camera, is normally considered, in its class, on a par with Leica (I have successfully used a Thirties' Rolleiflex for the past ten years). But it is a simpler mechanism, with a large format, $2\frac{1}{4}$in x $2\frac{1}{4}$in, and doesn't carry the cachet of its miniature German confrère. A No. 1 Rolleiflex (1928) will make no more than £40 ($100) in the saleroom. And, surprisingly, considering the vast numbers of enthusiasts, Rollei accessories are poor under-the-hammer performers: a kit to convert from 12 frames to 16 using a standard 120 film may fetch only £15-£20 (about $40). A Rollei collector, says David Allison of Christie's, could equip himself at a modest cost through auction buying. I would tip specialist Rolleis as the better performers for the future. The wide-angle Rollei (1961), with 55mm short focus lenses or the Tele-Rollei (1959), with 135mm long focus lenses are both worth watching.

It would be a mistake to think, though, that only "modern" cameras are within range of the small collector or tyro dealer. The majority of field cameras are in a fairly modest price bracket. For less than £100 ($250) an attractive mahogany frame Thornton Pickard quarter- or whole-plate field camera such as the Imperial could be purchased. A field camera is simply a camera designed to be used out of doors. Tropical field cameras were sometimes made of teak and these fetch normally over £200 ($500). Always remove the focusing screen and hold the camera up to a bright light to check for holes in the bellows. Working inside the bellows, you can often successfully tape up light leaks, however.

Using cut film, not glass plates, field cameras are eminently usable, and it is a fact that such cameras produced many of the finest images. Contrary to popular belief, it was not slow lenses that hindered early work in poor light; it was the slowness of the film: some plates would rate no higher than 8 ASA today. Pre-1880 wet plate cameras are in a different bracket, with prices rising to several thousand. Quite apart from characteristic details of construction, a wet plate can often be identified by the protective waxing and purple staining which sometimes has affected the wood of the case. Many wet plate cameras were of bellows construction: a sliding box design is a sure sign of a valuable pre-1880 wet plate camera.

Novelties and miniature cameras have considerable charm — and a strong following. On the first rung you might find the pretty little Coronet "Midget", a camera from the 1930s manufactured in mottled Bakelite. Collectors try to complete a run of all the seven or so shades produced. A Mycro 3 novelty camera, looking like a scaled down 35mm camera, comes complete with cute little ever-ready case. Another small-scale camera, a minor masterpiece of miniaturization, is the Compass, a British camera designed by Pemberton Billing in 1937. Although it is no bigger than the average light meter, it has a built-in coupled rangefinder, light meter, roll film back. In what must by now be a British tradition—ingenuity of design allied to arthritic methods of manufacture—the Compass needed to be made in Switzerland, by Lecoultre, the watchmaking firm. In truth, the Compass was no tool for the hamfisted, whose fingers could easily slip over the lens, and only 4,000 were made. Good news for to-day's owner, however: in 1978 the asking price for this rarity was £200 - £300 ($500-$700); today that can be doubled.

More recent oddities include the Periflex, a budget-priced precursor of the single lens reflex camera. Using a cylindrical "periscope", it was possible to view and focus through the lens. The spring-loaded device would whisk out of the way before the exposure, but it needed to be engaged for each shot — making fast work furious work.

So-called "detective" cameras are avidly sought, and often go unrecognized because of the disguise that was an essential part of their construction. After 1889, when the Eastman company devised a method of dry film photography using sensitized celluloid, all sorts of bizarre variations on the classic box shape began to be realized.

In the walking-stick camera the lens was at the tip of the crook of the stick, while the film wound round pulleys inside the handle. There were also cameras disguised as field glasses, books, hats, and more. The Fallowfield Facile looked like a piece of hand luggage, in fact it was a camera with a discreet release for the shutter. A walking-stick camera made £3,400 ($8,500) at a recent London auction, and waistcoat cameras by Stirns — they fix to a flat metal plate held against the midriff, the lens revealed through a button hole — are rapidly increasing in appeal and worth. The Pistolgraph, a camera with a pistol grip, dating to 1856, (worth several thousand today) was more trouble than it was worth for its inventor, Thomas Skaife. When he leveled his camera to take a shot of Queen Victoria in a procession he was promptly arrested as an assassin!

Carpentry tools

The earliest tools were made, not by some impersonal manufacturing company, but by the worker himself. A good tool was passed down from father to son, from master to apprentice. Handling an old drill, plane, adze or saw, you are somehow close to history. Collectors feel that the gloss on the wood, the gleam on the steel or brass, have been put there by hard work and sweat from the brow. The hobbyist or craftsman has a further bonus: he can use them.

Hobbyist collectors have been the most ardent supporters of the many auctions and tool dealers' shops that have sprung up over the past five or six years. Certain tools have a uniqueness of use that mark them out both as collector's items and do-it-yourself man's dream come true. At Jack Bittner's tool auction unusual molding planes were at a premium, especially one used to shape the edges of a drop leaf table, a frequent point of repair and an invaluable aid for the making of fine reproduction pieces. Signatures or other accredited maker's marks turn even quite ordinary tools into the holy grail; local people's work will always find a good price, as was evidenced by a $50 bid recently for a single plane by Cabot, a Vermont planemaker.

Part of the fun of collecting carpenter's tools is trying to work out what the implements of a clogger, cobbler or a cooper were actually used for. You may have heard of an adze, for instance, but do you know how it looks, what it was used for or how? Picture an adze like this: cup your hand, then turn your cupped hand down toward your wrist. Imagine your hand to be the iron or steel adze head with your fingertips, not the nails, as the cutting edge. An adze could be used to smooth planks laid down on a floor where it was not practical to use a plane.

Another ancient tool that is a variant of a familiar implement today is the side-axe. The side-axe looks like a fireman's axe but in fact only one side, the outside, of the blade was sharpened. The heel of the blade, not the handle, would be held in the hand, with the unsharpened side towards the body. The axe-man would chip away to shape and trim his work at uncanny speed. Coopers were adept with the side-axe. The cooper would "list" or shape staves at lightning speed with deft strokes of his side-axe by standing them on the ground or flinging them in the air. So true was his eye that when each stave was forced against its neighbor by the metal hoops of the barrel, a perfect watertight join would be created, without caulking or tonguing and grooving.

A large saw rather like a fretsaw in appearance, with several fine blades running parallel to each other, was for cutting veneers by hand. At one time the only way to slice a freshly-felled tree trunk into planks was to use a pit-saw. The pit-saw was often a segment of toothed steel about six feet long, and each end had a double-handed grip. One man straddled the tree trunk, laid horizontal on a high framework, and held one end of the pit-saw. His mate below held the other end. It was gruelling seesaw work, but there was no other way to do it.

Dating and identifying tools is a challenge to the amateur sleuth. On some wooden planes, for example, the maker's mark is on the front or toe end and will be positioned symmetrically. If a dealer's stamp has been added it will be clear of the maker's imprint. The owner, however, might impress his name or initials anywhere. One way of dating tools is to allow 30 years for the working life of each owner. Thus three sets of initials could indicate that a tool is at least 90 years old. Sometimes a date will be found. But this could indicate no more than the date of purchase or acquisition by a new owner. Further clues to dating may be found in the style of letters or bordering as there were clearly indentifiable typographical vogues over the years. The presence of old screws can mislead, as many long-established workshops kept a supply from the Dark Ages, so an old screw could have been used to replace a worn one in a contemporary tool.

Although tools are a relatively new field for the collector, the interest was started in the 1890s by a Norwegian doctor and was powerfully reinforced by Henry C. Mercer of Pennsylvania in the 1920s and by many other eminent American collectors. In recent years it has grown enormously. Scholarly research by W.L. Goodman of Bristol, England, and others has demonstrated that many of the old tools lying in disused basement workshops, and even at the bottom of your local repair man's work box, have a precise and traceable history back to the beginning of the 18th century; before that most workmen made their own wooden tools.

The pastime was given a popular boost in 1979 when Roy Arnold and Philip Walker, hobbyist-dealers in early tools, decided to dissolve their five-year partnership and put some 1,000 lots up for auction. The 6,000 18th and 19th century items included a Holtzapffel lathe and other ornamental turning apparatus; planes by Wooding, Jennion, Cogdell, Fitkin, Phillipson, and many other authenticated 18th century makers; a 36-piece set of hollows and rounds, side-snipes, side-rounds and snipe-bills; camera makers, air-tight case makers, and other special purpose planes. There was also a remarkable series of broad axes, adzes, twybills and other edged tools; iron, steel and bronze planes by Spiers, Norris, Price and Towell; braces and saws of all types as well as fitted and veneered tool chests — highly desirable as the tools, if present, having been protected down the years, are often of the highest quality and perfectly preserved.

As part of their operation the partners had produced a series of beautifully illustrated sales catalogs; the catalogs themselves — *The Traditional Tools of the Carpenter and other Craftsmen* — are covetable items today and form part of the standard literature. When I met Arnold Walker I asked him what the best way was to go about collecting. Grouping tools is a problem, he said: "One is inclined to put together all the metal tools, or associate tools with a similar function — like drilling or planing. But I should prefer to arrange them under nationalities or trades if this were possible."

The trade that the partners found most appealing for its variety and virtuosity was that of the wheelwright; "He was the wainwright (making the whole wagon as well as the wheels), the house carpenter, the joiner, the coffin maker (coffin planes are a grisly but interesting little bywater of the hobby), the turner and many other things besides, while the close association between a blacksmith and farrier often made him a fair hand at working iron as well."

Nevertheless, such fastidious collecting may prove impractical, and the tyro will be better advised to choose a basic implement, like the plane. The plane has a long history — some 2,000 years — and both wooden and metal planes are known from the earliest days: 11 Roman metal planes still survive. Apparently there are three reasons why metal often had the edge on wood for planes. First, the sole needed extra strength to prevent excessive wear; then the cutting iron was wont to split a wooden plane when it was driven in and a metal lining prevented this; finally, a metal screw device eventually made it possible to adjust the cutting iron.

In the 1860s Bailey's various mechanisms appeared in the US enabling mechanical adjustment of the cutter, and by the beginning of this century American pattern planes had established a hold on the international mass market for their ease of use and low cost, although not necessarily their durability — as witness the number of cracked and elaborately repaired examples in old tool kits. As one hopeful tool collector said, theoretically at least, it could happen that a master carpenter would be repairing a Chippendale cabinet with the same tool originally used to make it!

There is a lot of helpful material for the carpentry tool collector to read. *American Axes,* by Kauffman, *Early American Tools,* by Gault (with price guide) and *Tools That Built America,* by Bealer, are all worth seeing. The illustrated catalog of the Arnold & Walker sale, *Traditional Tools of the Carpenter and other Craftsmen,* is a scholarly work with numerous illustrations. There are two high priests of the specialty: W.L. Goodman, author of *The History of Woodworking Tools* and *British Planemakers from 1700,* and R.A. Salaman, who wrote the introduction to the Arnold Walker sale catalog and the now famous *Dictionary of Tools Used in the Woodworking and Allied Trades.*

Early erotica: the collectable pin-up

Today's collector of early erotica looks round the bookstalls and is saddened. Everywhere he sees explicit pin-up pictures, everywhere a desperate attempt to cudgel the senses to a reaction. Curiously, now that sex isn't naughty anymore its depiction has suddenly (or so it seems) become a deadly serious affair, with profit the name of the game. So where has all the fun gone? According to keen collector Celestino Valenti, "Contemporary pin-ups give too much away. There's not enough fun or suggestion." He hoards every type of erotic ephemera from 19th century photographic postcards and 18th century etchings to film magazines of the Forties and Fifties. "It's true that a lot of film fan magazines are coy, and corny even, but many collectors prefer understatement; they like the cheesecake look!"

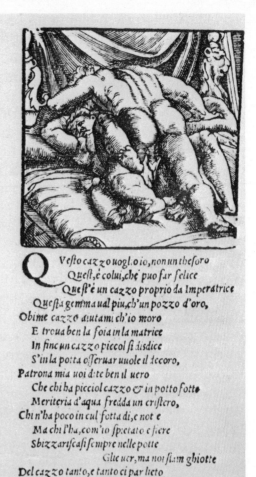

Mettimi uu dito iu cul caro uecchione
  E ſpingi dentro il cazzo apoco apoco
Alza ben queſta gamba,e fa buon gioco
Poi mena ſenza far reputatione;
Che per mia fè qdeſto è,miglior boccone
  Che mangiar il pan unto apreſſo il foco
  E s'in potta ti ſpiacc,muta loco
C'huomo non è, chi non è bugcrone;
In potta io ue'l farò queſta fiata,
  E,in cul queſt'altra,e'n potta,e'n culo il cazzo
  Me fara lieto, c uoi lieta, e beata;
E chi uol eſſer gran maeſtro e pazzo
  Che proprio e un uccel perde giornata
  Che d'altro,che di fotter ha ſoiazzo,
                              E crepi nel palazzo
Ser cortigiano,& aſpetti, che'l tal moya,
  Ch'io per me penſo ſol trarmi la ſoia

Queſto cazzo uogl.o io,non un theſoro
  Queſt,è colui,che puo far felice
  Queſt'è un cazzo proprio da Imperatrice
Queſta gemma ual piu,ch'un pozzo d'oro,
Obime cazzo aiutami ch'io moro
  E troua ben la ſoia in la matrice
  In fine un cazzo piccol ſi diſdice
S'in la potta oſſeruar uuole il decoro,
Patrona mia uoi dite ben il uero
  Che chi ha picciol cazzo & in potto fotte
  Meriteria d'aqua fredda un criſtero,
Chi n'ha poco in cul fotta di,e not e
  Ma chi l'ha,com'io ſpietato e ſiere
  Sbizzariſcaſi ſempre nelle potte
                              Glie ucr,ma noi ſiam ghiotte
Del cazzo tanto,e tanto ci par lieto
  Che terremmo la guglia innanzi e drite

Extracts from an erotica book with woodcut illustrations by Pietro Aretino (probably before November 1527). Sold by Christie's New York in 1978.

At the top of the price list is period erotica: wasp-waisted nudes draped over penny farthing bicycles; or, even earlier, lusty lords in pomaded wigs, grappling with their partners in etched ecstasy on four poster beds. Sometimes the otherwise naked frolicking aristos still have on their quaint little silver-buckled shoes...

Right down the price scale and within easy grasp of the novitiate collector are the movie magazines. Many old American ones spotlight today's well-known film stars revealing their all — or a close second to it — in a desperate bid to attract the eye of the casting director. Because the framed covers make attractive wall decor, such magazines now change hands for several dollars an issue. Titles to look for are: *Pin-up*, *Wink* (subtitled, *The Whirl of a Girl*), *Outdoor Antics*, *Beauty Parade*, *Eyeful*, *High Heel*, *Titter*, *Movie Humor*, *Movie Merrygoround* and *Reel Humor*. Certain British girlie books — especially those dating from World War II are equally collectable. The *David Wright Portfolio* contains many fine color plates of fancifully dressed and half-dressed lovelies. Another wartime publication ex-servicemen may recall with nostalgic relish is *Victory*. Describing itself as *'The Weekly for India Command'*, it cost "Tommy" eight annas a copy.

The psychologists and sociologists have tried to explain the lure of the pin-up, as everything else. The girls in the pictures they claim are paradoxically "available"; they can be studied at leisure, paraded; but, unlike wives and lovers, they don't answer back. But no-one has ever fully explained the fascination with Victorian and Georgian pin-ups. There is certainly a strong element of nostalgia born of the irrefutable knowledge that the lovely young creatures depicted not only lost their look and charms in the folds and wrinkles of old age, but they are now to be found beneath daisies — a poignant reminder to us all. However, it was the need, healthy and vigorous, to enjoy life while we could that surely led to the birth of the very earliest pictures that can truly be called pin-ups. It began in about the middle of the last century in France. The typical female image was the *grisette* or actress, inevitably a mistress. Always "resting", she would be seen luxuriating in her bath, draped over a silky bed, arranging her feathers or worrying about her poses and her lovers. The typical woman of the day tended to be a heavy-set creature, not at all the svelte form we have become accustomed to as our mannequins. Yet thanks to the Press, idealization was at hand. *La Vie Parisienne*, a magazine that appeared in 1862, dealt with plays and exhibitions, gossip and so on; but, most of all, in its fine line drawings and elegant colored covers, launched onto an unsuspecting world the *idea* of the Parisian woman, as a beautiful "woman icon" for the rest of the Western world.

Among the almost forgotten popular artists and illustrators of the era - Robida, Bac and Gerbalt — it was R. De La Nezière who contributed most to the *fin de siècle* issue of *La Vie Parisienne*. Mars and Grevin Gavarni are artists associated with another much sought after contemporary publication *Le Journal Amusant*. In the Art Nouveau period, the lines and arabesques of the female form inspired designs for everything from paper knives to mirrors and the facades of

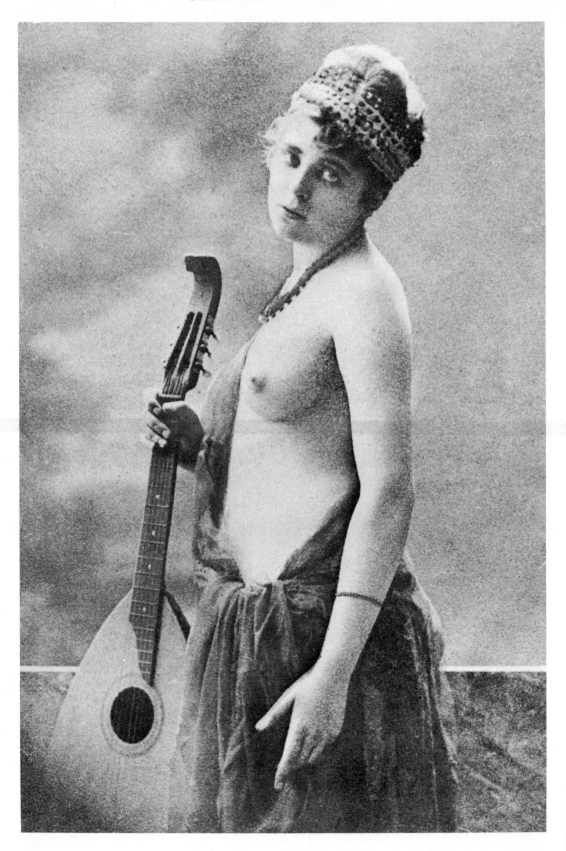

important buildings; elegant, sensual, Art Nouveau woman was always tastefully depicted.

Like many collectors, Valenti covets Mucha's woman, splendid even postcard-size. No-one could express the decorative madness of Art Nouveau so well as Mucha. But Valenti refuses to pay silly prices for postcards. Other artists whose names and monograms collectors seek are Hérouard and Kirchner, Gerda Wegener (one of the few women with a talent for drawing women), Wilette, Fabiano and Brunelleschi.

From the First World War years, collectors search for magazines like *Le Rire Rouge, Fantasio* and *La Baionette* (a title with a slightly disturbing *double entendre*). After the war, *Le Rire Rouge* became *Le Rire; La Vie Parisienne* remained, but *Monsieur,* a forerunner of *Playboy* and *Lui,* folded. The work of Hérouard and Maurice Millière in the pages of *La Vie Parisienne* must have provided an inspirational backdrop for that most famous of the pin-up artists, and a wizard with an air-brush, Vargas. His work first appeared in 1920, and his well-built, all-American conception of scantily-clad beauty soon earned him a huge following and a lifelong association with *Esquire* magazine which gave way to *Playboy* in the Sixties.

Deco collectors are rediscovering the vivid and fanciful ladies that French graphic artist Louis Icart created in the 1920s and 1930s. Leda and the Swan (1934) shows a languidly reclining nude, one arm around the brooding black swan that dominates two thirds of the etching and drypoint design. Her face shows more an expression of come-on than coyness or fear. Icart's leggy ladies and their flimsy attire often blend with the design. In one, a nude rises from the smoke of a cigarette; in another, the famous L'Elan, a fleet-of-foot demoiselle, naked, runs with fantastic hounds out of a sensual confusion of chiffon, animal fur and the whipping wind.

Jean Schmitt of Golden Griffins, New Hope, Pennsylvania described Icart as the "Tiffany of Art Deco". Curiously, the out and out naked ladies are now coming back into popularity in the US: when they first became available to the decorator trade in the early Twenties, it was the *implied* nudity that struck a chord in the American psyché. Icart had his first American exhibition in the gallery of John Wanamaker's New York department store in 1922. After that Icart never could put a foot wrong Stateside. Today's collectors are researching Icart book illustrations, fashion drawings and cheaper editions, for even the least successful of his genre etchings will rate a $500 (£200) price tag.

Getting stuck into bayonets

The bayonet owes its name to the town of Bayonne in France. The town was famous for a type of knife and, so the story goes, it was in the 17th century that the fighting folk of Bayonne had the bright idea of thrusting the hilts of their knives into the empty barrels of their muskets, so turning a useless piece of artillery into a long and lethal type of instant pike! The problem was that early fire-arms were one-shot weapons and re-loading was a dangerous and lengthy procedure. While the musketeer was inserting the charge and ramming home the shot he was a sitting target. In the 17th century pike-men guarded musketeers, but the Bayonne idea was too good not to be speedily adopted and vigorously developed.

Probably the earliest known bayonets in common use date to c.1660. A typical "plug" bayonet, as they were known, has a blade that is broad at the base and tapers to a point. A cross-guard is common, and some have a fuller (groove in the blade) and a wavy cutting edge. The tips of the cross-guard, often of brass, can take the form of human heads or "angels". The grip may well be polished wood also capped in brass. Sentimental or patriotic slogans sometimes adorn the blade, and bespoke bayonets may be rather more elaborate, with ivory grips and splendidly carved quillons (hand guard or cross-pieces), cross-guard and pommel.

Clearly, however, the plug idea was good in an emergency but a liability long-term. The plug bayonet might be inserted, by accident, before the musket had been fired. Then pulling the trigger might — at the very least — obliterate the bayonet! Or it might be impossible to remove the plugged bayonet and no more shots could be fired. By the 18th century the method of attachment had improved considerably; the bayonet now had a tube-like fitting which slotted over the outside of the muzzle. This locked into position (rather like a bayonet socket lamp, hence the description) and it allowed the musket to be fired even with the bayonet in position. Bayonets were carried in a sheath suspended from a cross-belt.

The blade of a plug bayonet usually bears the armorer's mark; a wolf or king's head stamp denotes German steel. The socket bayonet, which to begin with had almost no handle, merely a steel ring, featured a long and elegant blade, some as long as a short sword. Some also have a fuller — the groove on the blade that reduces its weight. Plug bayonets are rare, and those that were later converted to the socket style are rarer still and highly collectable.

The French sabre-type bayonet is the best looking of all. The single-edged blade undulate's slightly and extends 22½ inches beyond its five inch handle. The handle is brass with horizontal grooves to act as a grip. Along the back of the blade will be found engraved in flowery script the date and maker's name. Several years ago I came across such a sabre at an antiques maket. It seemed a bargain; however, its silver metal scabbard was missing, and bayonet collectors are perfectionists when it comes to matching bayonets with their original scabbards.

Blade variations make an interesting specialized study in bayonets. After 1800 there is sometimes a reinforced armor-piercing tip on socket bayonets, while the blade of the Mauser (German) rifle bayonet, 1914-18 issue, sometimes has a row of fearsome saw-teeth along the back of the blade. German Mauser bayonets have gone up in price from the early Seventies; German weapons are always collectable, but similar advances have been seen with British bayonets.

The most recent type of bayonet, still in use today, is the spring bayonet. The hilt is grooved and carries a spring device that locks on to a protrusion on the rifle or machine-gun barrel. The most easily accessible bayonet, price-wise, is the one known as the pig-sticker. These were issued during World War II and resemble nothing so much as the device on the boy scout's jack-knife that is meant to remove stones from horses' hooves. Ugly, but light in weight, these were nonetheless effective for skewering the enemy and also ideal for putting holes into cans of sweetened milk! Pig-stickers can be found in their tubular scabards, usually very heavily greased, and will not make too much of a dent in the household budget.

At the top end of the range are the German dress model bayonets issued in the last two wars. The pommels, of heavy metal, are usually shaped like an eagle's head; and the handle has plastic or wooden grips decorated with a checkered non-slip pattern. The single-edged blade can be blued or bright plated and often features a swastika or imperial eagle emblem (pre-Republic). Geoffrey Warner, consultant to an international militaria specialist firm, told me: "Third Reich Nazi weapons are at a premium now; but condition is of prime importance." He says you should never clean a pitted and scarred blade for fear of removing the blueing or maker's marks.

Aside from the detachable bayonet that needed to be seperately installed in the rifle, there are combination weapons in which the bayonet is an integral part of the barrel. Here, the bayonet is fixed rather like a form of flick-knife. The bayonet is hinged and bent back, so forcing itself against a spring: the point is locked in place by a slide or catch which can be released by a trigger mechanism. When this occurs, the blade flicks forward and automatically locks in place. Such weapons are known from as early as 1680, but the idea was not patented until 1781 by John Waters. By the end of the 18th century spring bayonets were common attachments to blunderbusses and pistols. Generally the blade is of hollow-ground triangular section; it can be found on top of, or at the side of, or underneath the barrel. Even pocket pistols meant for personal defence sometimes feature this intriguing type of last-ditch edged weapon. Curiously, however, there is very little record of these spring-loaded bayonets ever being used. Draw your own conclusions!

Arctophily: the art of collecting teddy bears

I have been an arctophile for many years — but it took me a long while to realize it. I still own, love, and look after the teddy bear that my long-dead grandpa gave me 35 years ago. (An arctophile is a teddy bear collector; from the Greek *arktos,* bear, and *philos,* friend or lover.)

I don't remember why my bear's ears fell off (maybe they were encouraged to by small fingers). But I do know that my grandmother sewed on cute little pointed ones as replacements. And I do remember feeding the bear, now almost bald all over his body, with pastry I had made alongside my mother in the kitchen: which accounts for his pursed, hand-stitched lips (no-one need ever tell my bear to button his lip!). And I do recall the tug of war with the boy in the next bed in the convalescent home during which both I and the bear lost our heads. Only the bear had his stitched back on by an obliging nurse.

The bear has always been an acceptable toy for a boy; for a start, he is a hardier creature than a doll, being invariably naked (although mine still wears some of my sister's old dolls' cast-offs!). And instead of that "ma-ma" stuff, some of the best bears actually growled when they were so inclined.

Another plus point for the male teddy bear hunter is his quarry's clear-cut masculine origin. In 1902, a cartoon by Clifford Berryman appeared in the *Washington Post.* It showed President Theodore

(Teddy) Roosevelt with a small brown bear cub lying at his feet: Roosevelt had refused to shoot it. So the story goes, the President had gone south to settle a boundary dispute between states, and his reluctance to shoot the bear was an indication of his fair minded attitude, expressed as a political allegory. Thereafter the bear became a symbol associated with the President.

Shrewd Brooklyn candy store owner Morris Michtom got his wife, a toymaker, to produce a brown plush bear to take advantage of the association and, having obtained permission from the President, nicknamed it "Teddy's Bear". The teddy bear craze had begun.

Michtom, a Russian immigrant, was able to capitalize on his creation and eventually founded the Ideal Toy Corporation, one of the biggest toy companies in the US. Michtom's plush teddy bears have button eyes (my bear lost his eyes in a game of doctors and nurses about 30 years ago and has eyes made of buttons. The cross stitching makes him look cross-eyed).

The teddy bear craze gave rise to a number of quips, such as the cheeky comment that Lily Langtry, King Edward VII's bosom companion, preferred her Teddy, bare, and an American version that went: "If Theodore is President of the United States with his clothes on what is he with his clothes off? A Teddy Bare." The Germans also lay claim to an early involvement with teddy bears, in the form of the toys produced by the Margarethe Steiff toy firm, founded in the 1880s. Steiff teddies are very desirable and easy to recognize by their ear buttons (*Knopf im Ohr*, button in ear, became the company's trademark). Steiff bears also feature long arms, paws that turn in, a humped back and button eyes. Steiff bears have short snouts, but the above characteristics, together with a long snout, could also indicate an early bear. Big feet are another sign of an old teddy (humps went out in c.1908, by the way).

Shoebutton eyes — shoebuttons were in plentiful supply before the First World War — are another pointer to old age. The intriguingly named Fast Black Skirt Company produced an "Electric Bright Eye" teddy whose eyes lit up when the right paw was shaken. A 1914 patented bear by Louis Schiffer of New York was Janus-faced: one side of the head had a bear's face, the other a bisque-headed doll's face, the body being plush and bear-like in the classic furry tradition. Today this is reckoned a real gem.

Mechanical bears are coveted cuddlies, as are the very large bears (often with diminutive heads), which may have been a studio photographer's prop to coax children into a suitably disarming pose. Peter the bear was a particularly ferocious looking creature, with rolling eyes, long teeth and a big tongue, made by the Gebrueder Sussenguth factory in Thuringia in the late 1920s. British doll dealer Carol Ann Stanton managed to buy almost the entire stock, still boxed, of a closed-down toy shop in Germany. There appears to have been around a hundred variations of Peter bear, all of them guaranteed to have scared the pants off the kids — which may have accounted for the shop having gone out of business...

Walking sticks, travelers' tricks

Perhaps the least exciting walking sticks, to the collector, are those expressly designed for their true purpose — to help you walk. Typical country sticks are made of blackthorn or ash; dried and varnished kale sticks — strong and unusually light — were a Scottish favorite. Officers in Highland regiments often preferred the stick to the traditional rattan cane, favoring walking sticks embellished with their regimental crests. But here you are into the province of the militaria fancier and must expect the appropriate price hike.

Some walking sticks turn out to be swordsticks — always give the handle a sharp twist and a tug; you may discover a rapier thin blade (possibly of Spanish steel) concealed in the wooden shaft. Towards the end of the 18th century swords hanging from the belt went out of fashion — but villains did not, and a swordstick, in normal circumstances a lethal gimmick, could turn into a lifesaver.

"The Unknown World of Canes", an exhibition held in Paris in 1980, spotlighted some of the fierce and fascinating variations on the sword theme. One swordstick had sprung-loaded quillons that flicked into place the instant the handle with its rapier blade was withdrawn. The quillons are the crosspiece that protect your hand from your opponent's sword. Knifesticks were also in evidence, with spring-loaded blades appearing at the top or bottom of an innocuous looking cane. Some sticks feature a pistol concealed in the hand grip: it was a decorous way of carrying a gun when smartly dressed. Or the cane shaft itself may be the barrel of a powerful air gun — a favorite "tool" of the poacher — or even a shotgun.

Especially desirable are the dual purpose swordsticks, gun and blade combined. The idea dated from the time when a fire-arm could not be quickly reloaded (or relied upon to fire first time!) and it made sense to fashion the weapon in the shape of brass knuckles or to have a knife blade attached to the barrel as a back-up or fail-safe weapon.

However, wandering weapon-stick fanciers should beware. One American who bought a swordstick in London forgot to declare it at Heathrow airport. It was revealed by the metal detector and confiscated. In the States walking with a swordstick is illegal. In the UK it is permissable to carry one but against the law to use it, while in West Germany mere possession is a crime.

A little less drastic is the whip stick or bludgeon stick, both self-explanatory and rarer still than the swordstick. Positively benign was the walking stick dating to 1785, the handle of which revealed a candleholder and reflector to light the way home before the introduction of street lamps.

Because the handle of a walking stick forms a natural beak shape to fit the hand it was a short step for the cane maker to carve the grip into the beak of a bird or the snout of a dog; people-shaped pommels are also known and keenly collected. The cane handle could be the wood of the shaft or separately made of porcelain, gunmetal, pinchbeck, brass, bronze, glass, mother of pearl, tortoiseshell, ivory, bone, gold or silver (the hallmark will give an exact date, to add to the value).

The walking stick habit started in the 16th century and declined only at the outbreak of World War I. Although a fine cane was the mark of a well-dressed man-about-town, in the late 17th century, fashionable ladies of that period also toted canes. Indeed, from 1750 to about 1800, heels were so high and walking on them so hazardous, that carrying a cane became less of an accessory and more of a necessity!

Delicate filigree worked ivory tapped canes of the 1700s are now highly prized and priced. Much more accessible to the beginning collector are the novelty canes of the 19th century and later. Look for those in which the grip unscrews to reveal a pipe or spirit flask for a surreptitious smoke or swig. Handles concealed money compartments, snuff boxes, compasses, opera glasses; the shaft could be a telescope tube or hide a fishing line.

A brush with shaving history

Barbers occasionally get hooked on the paraphernalia of their own trade and sport a display of shaving mugs in the window. If they grow tired of their "shaviana" show you may be able to pick up a ready made collection on the cheap. Shaving mugs seem to have been missed by the masses and you could comb the shops and markets and form a definitive collection today for a modest sum.

Prices of individual pieces vary with age and design. A fairly plain Thirties' mug might sell for a few notes. Transfer printed mugs dating from 1910 to 1930 should go no higher than a tenner, but may cost more if the transfer decoration depicts a known event or famous monument. A date will also turbocharge the price.

Attractive shaving mugs come in the form of a dolphin or fantastic

sea beast. The genuine early dolphin mug — 1860 to 1900 — is finely potted; the shaver filled it with hot water and dipped his brush into the gaping mouth. But beware: there have been reproductions, though the bright coloration is a giveaway once you have become familiar with the more subtle hues our 19th century ancestors favored. Bird and elephant shapes were a turn-of-the-century craze and dog and cat heads are also known.

At the top end of the market are anthropomorphic shave mugs, those depicting Boer War generals being avidly sought. A mug meant as a gift may carry an appealing endearment; named mugs are also desirable. Truefitt's, the rather grand old style barber shop in London's Old Bond Street (part of the collection of which is photographed on these pages), say that any man worth his salt kept a named mug at the barber's reserved for his personal use.

Curiously, potters' marks are rarely found on shaving mugs, and it is thought that they were a low price item originally imported from Germany.

Corkscrews - a new twist on an old theme

Corkscrews always seemed to me to fit into one of two categories: those that worked efficiently, which I quickly forgot about, and those irritating specimens that fell down on the job — and forced me to wait to get at the glorious juice of the grape. Now I discover there is much more to it than that: there are some 2,000 types and corkscrews are beginning to fetch heady prices at auction. Individual corkscrews have been known to fetch as much as $750 (£300) and more. But you can still buy interesting, attractive (and useable) specimens for the price of a few gallons of gas.

Corking was introduced in the 17th century. The screw part of the corkscrew is almost always of steel, though the handle can be precious metal, such as silver; nicely turned bone or even a wooden handle is also desirable. Some screws have a useful brush sticking out at the side of the handle.

Almost all worthwhile corkscrews were made before 1920; novelty types date from the 1890s and feature built-in extras like can openers, bottle openers, pocket knives, wire cutters, and so on. Gimmicky corkscrews in the lower price range include those that link up with a favorite sport: a horse's head, golf balls or a cricket bat may feature. Rather more desirable would be one with a glass handle decorated like the famous mille fiori paperweights, with tiny colored glass flowers seen through the clear glass covering.

Warren Rowe, chief of the International Correspondence of Corkscrew Addicts, enthuses about the ingenious patent examples with levers and subsidiary screw mechanisms, designed to raise the cork as neatly and painlessly as possible. Corkscrews range from the simple T-shape or gimlet type, to the ingenious patent corkscrews with levers and subsidiary screws. The wine bar type corkscrew attaches to the counter and the cork is released with a pump action not unlike that used to draw a pint of beer from the wood in a traditional British pub.

The "penny blacks" of corkscrew collecting are those made by Robert Jones. They have a plain brass shaft, are about half an inch in diameter and have a bone handle — plus a brush to flick away those vintage cobwebs. One went at auction recently for £390 ($950): it was the first of a registered design and dated to 1840. Silver corkscrews can cost even more. Sometimes a corkscrew has other attachments built in, such as a nutmeg grater, or pipe tamper.

All sorts of people are interested in corkscrews. The International Correspondence numbers hospital porters, a professor of medicine, an architect, a designer. Sadly there is a waiting list, and membership is limited to 50 throughout the world. But you could write to Mr. Rowe for more information (or if you have a corkscrew to sell or exchange) at 25 St. Edmund's Avenue, Ruislip, Middlesex, England.

6

Collector In The Kitchen

Change came slowly to the 19th century kitchen because servants were plentiful and cheap. Thanks to kitchen gadgets, grinding, mixing, freezing, toasting and roasting are plug-in activities we take for granted today. Without such labor-saving devices, life must have been a dreadful drudge. Cook made do with an array of wood and metal utensils and some often quite efficient prototype gadgets. But there is no need to be a cook to appreciate the rustic charms of cooking curiosa: many of the pieces make excellent ornaments or room decoration. An old wooden butter churn, for example, gleamingly varnished, with its metal parts picked out in bright paint and bedecked with a sheaf of dried flowers.

The best bread board examples come in cherry wood and boxwood. Look for beautiful carved leaf and fruit designs, also for wooden butter pats and cake molds(slabs of carved wood which would be impressed into the soft dough before baking). As with bread boards, European origin wooden implements are often the most striking. And there are a host of other items to watch for, like apple scoops, bottle openers, coffee mills, ice picks, meat jacks, scales and balances, and mechanical aids, such as the Spong patent knife cleaner. Of late 19th century vintage, this consists of brushes which rotate inside a large wooden drum fixed in a cast iron frame. Knives were inserted in holes on top; when the crank was turned, the brushes moved against the cutlery and, hopefully, cleaned it.

Actually Mr. Spong was an amazing man; inside 35 years his company had filed nearly 100 patents for gadgets. He designed a mincer able to chew up a whole whale, a freezing machine to turn water into "pure ice"; he was also the first to create the cast iron mincer which clamped to the edge of a table, as well as a number of rotary cutters and fruit and vegetable slicers. The chief cook at Buckingham Palace, Mr. John Hutin, wrote to James Spong in 1868: "Your Mincing Machines which I have used in the Palace, answer admirably in every way."

Tea caddies

The Chinese sent their tea to Europe in crude zinc containers. With these they sent small holders known as *kati,* hence the term, caddy. The original kati held about 1⅓ lb and that measure was kept for caddies for many hundreds of years. Hand-painted Chinese bottles were much admired and often sent to silversmiths to be gilded or mounted with silver edging. A silver knop (knob) might be added to cheer up the porcelain bottle stopper.

Glass tea caddies are also known. Perhaps the most famous of these are the opaque white glass bottles believed to have been made in South Staffordshire, England, from 1755-60. The early Staffs specimens are gorgeously decorated with enamel flowers, song birds and the names of the teas they contained: Green, Black, Hyson or Bohea. Tea caddies are known in silver, porcelain, glass, wood, ivory, papier mâché, pewter. The brightly enameled, pressed tinplate caddies that were issued in great numbers to commemorate coronations and suchlike over the last 100 years are popular with newcomers to caddy collecting. But they are the bottom end of the market. The most interesting examples are those dating to the time when tea was a precious commodity, and caddies had locks fitted to prevent pilferage by servants.

Silver caddies made in the reigns of Kings George II and George III of England are usually rectangular or oval, with a flat top and bottom. Plain or elaborately chased, they were often made in matching pairs. And the best ones came complete in a snug-fitting shagreen – green-tinted sharkskin – covered case. The original Chinese kati was made of hard red stoneware and looked more like a whisky hip flask than a box. Later the Chinese made similar bottles in porcelain, and copied favorite English styles of decoration on to their porcelain tea bottles.

The Orientals also sent over "fruit" caddies; these were wood carved to look like a fruit. Soon English wood carvers were producing apple and pear shaped tea containers, complete with carved wood stalks on top. Aubergines are popular with collectors as they are a Chinese symbol of good luck, but cantaloup shapes are the rarest.

Egg cups

Our ancestors were great egg-eaters: hearty breakfasters could down as many as half a dozen eggs in a sitting. We also know that they ate a far greater variety of eggs. Tiny egg cups would in the 19th century almost certainly have contained bantam eggs. And the giant size receptacles were meant for turkey, goose and even swans' eggs.

Eggs were sometimes brought to the table in racks in a raw state and were cooked on the table to the eater's preferred consistency. Some large egg racks have a candle holder beneath—though this was possibly used to keep the eggs warm rather than cook them from raw.

The pottery or porcelain egg cup did not appear until the 17th century. Egg containers can also incorporate a space for condiments, toast and butter. A rare egg boiler from the reign of George III features a built-in hour-glass on top.

A silver egg cruet and spoons set.

The earliest form of single egg cup appears to be itself an hour-glass shape. As these were fragile, few survived. Early wooden egg cups, in a inverted bell shape, and sometimes with a commemorative message, were far sturdier. From around 1820 to 1840 there was a vogue for papier-mâché egg cups. These, in common with much of the furniture and occasional items, like tea trays, also feature interesting and finely worked inlaid mother of pearl. The porcelain firm of Goss created pretty, delicate and finely-potted egg cups featuring its typical and easily recognizable crest. Commemorative egg cups present the lower-priced end of the market. The most sought after Coronation egg cup would be one depicting the most famous short-term English monarch of all time: Edward VIII.

Silver, Sheffield plate or electroplate egg boilers are known; the boiler itself is usually no more than a cylindrical can with a small spirit lamp beneath. Inside is a pierced plate to hold the eggs. The best boilers are of beautifully wrought metal and have an egg timer mounted on the lid. Collectable ones have matching egg cups and egg spoons.

In the 1920s chromium-plated egg boilers were put onto the US market incorporating a bell which rang when the egg was boiled.

In the 1930s there was a vogue for egg cups in the form of animals and birds to encourage children to eat more eggs. Also desirable are egg cups from much closer to present times featuring familiar TV characters. If egg cups appear in pairs, buy both, and if they are part of a cruet set buy the complete set. And if you see an egg cup that is small on top and large at the bottom it probably means it was designed to take two kinds of eggs, big or small, depending on which bird had produced in the farmyard.

Spoons

With so many spoons to choose, some people specialize. Caddy spoons are a favorite. They come in many metals, shapes and sizes — you'll find them scalloped like a sea shell, in the form of a fish, a pair of hands, or a jockey's cap. First cousin to the caddy spoon is the mote skimmer, a flattened spoon with a perforated bowl and a sharply-pointed handle. When tea was a more rough and ready brew, the mote — twigs, grits and even insects — would float to the surface. The skimmer removed them and the sharp end cleared any blockage in the spout of the teapot.

A large brass, copper or tin spoon with holes in the bowl may be a soup skimmer, used from medieval times to remove the scum from soup. A pretty, delicately perforated spoon is probably a sugar sifter. Shovel-shaped spoons were used for salt, their bowls becoming rounded in later years. Watch for rare baby feeders; the bowl is enclosed so you can pour in the feed, and there's a hollow tube at the tip of the bowl for baby to suck.

Collectors pick up old spoons as they poke about in the bric-à-brac box you'll find in the corner of almost every antique shop. Smaller spoons for coffee, miniature ones for salt, and with an antique ladle you can sup in style on a can of soup. Another bonus for the spoon collector: you can use low-price silver specimens to gen up on the mysteries of hallmarking. If a spoon has been used parts of the hallmark may have been rubbed away. However, with a bit of detective work you can generally pin-point the date unless the "improver" has been at work. It was a common trick to jazz up old spoons in the last century: bright cut—an engraving technique that makes plain silver sparkle — may have been a later embellishment.

Forgeries are few but watch for fake Apostle and marrow spoons. Apostle spoons have a miniature effigy as an end knob to the handle and they were faked in quantity in the early 1900s. Marrow was a popular delicacy in the 18th and 19th centuries. People used long pointed spoons, with almost no bowl to speak of, to get at the marrow in bones. A cunning silversmith can turn a common dessert spoon into a rare marrow scoop.

Bottles

Many bottles were buried as rubbish; a prime garbage site has been known to yield as many as 10,000 bottles. But in such insalubrious surroundings bottles bearing original labels are understandably scarce. Labeled specimens occasionally come to light in an attic or cellar, or they can be purchased at a specialist dealer and carry a premium corresponding to rarity.

Why are old bottles so popular? Partly for decorative reasons. A selection of bottles in glittering blue, green, aqua, red, brown, gold, irridescent (due to the action of chemicals in the soil) or milky white glass is a surefire eye catcher. Stoneware bottles are another favorite; they were in general use almost until the last war, and contained vinegar and beers. The lustrous glaze on

Some two-tone, champagne shape British ginger beer bottles.

stoneware was hand applied. If you discover in the clay a telltale thumb print from a clumsy worker, this isn't a flaw—it only adds to the value and human interest.

The earliest ginger beer bottles usually bear the maker's mark impressed or incised into the soft mix before it is fired. Attractive two-tone bottles are plentiful: they may be russet brown or chestnut color down to the shoulder, with the body a pale creamy shade. Rare ginger beers are those that are green on top. Later ginger beers carry attractive transfer labeling giving the maker's name and address or an unusual trade mark. One collector goes for birds, fishes and insects.

The manufacturers of glass bottles and of earthenware bottles kept up a running battle between 1650 and 1850. The stone or earthenware bottle lost out when the demand for clear glass bottles became overwhelming. Not only was the customer becoming more fussy — wanting to see the color, quality and texture of what she was buying — but in addition, a nice glass bottle made life easier in the kitchen: the housewife or cook could see at a glance when supplies needed replenishing.

The earliest glass bottles were blown from a blob of molten glass. They have a "scar" of glass in the base caused by the pontil rod, which was dipped in molten glass to transport the embryo bottle for the finishing process. These first glass bottles couldn't stand straight and were sometimes placed in a basket-work cover rather like the modern-day Chianti wine bottle from Italy. At a later date the apprentice would press the pontil rod into the base of the bottle while the glass was still soft. This produced the "kick-up", an inverted dome which is still incorporated as a token gesture in many modern wine bottles. But it did enable the bottle to stand on its flattened base.

Corking was introduced in the early 1700s with the bulk import of port wine to England and it colonies. The wine matured in the bottle, which was kept on its side, the cork providing a leakproof fit.

The screw stopper was invented by Henry Barrett in 1872; a few years later came the "swing" stopper, similar to that found on many present-day mineral water or lemonade bottles. The crown cap was an 1892 invention. The old slow method of blowing glass and rolling it by hand gave way to blowing the glass into a wooden mold. By the middle of the 19th century all but the lip of the bottle could be made inside the mold, which by then was usually metal rather than wood. Because the mold was in two parts and hinged, there was usually a seam – a slight ridge of glass – along the sides of the bottle where the hot melt had oozed into the crack. The result is a useful dating guide for the modern collector. A rule of thumb timetable looks like this:

Up to 1860 – pontil mark on bottom of bottle;
mold seam ends low on neck or down on shoulder of bottle.
1860-1880 – mold seam ends below the mouth of bottle.
1890-1900 – mold seam usually within a quarter of an inch of top of bottle. Body, neck and lip are formed in the mold; only the top finished by hand.
1903 to present day – machine-made bottles. The mold seam extends the full length of the bottle.
1919 to present day – conventional screw-top bottles.

With the hinged mold came an added boon for traders: now special metal plates could be fitted inside the mold to emboss the glass and carry a selling slogan, advertise the maker's name or spell out a message. Sometimes the embossing letters were inserted individually. A letter missed out or put in back to front yielded errors which make the bottle worth at least twice as much.

To help make sense of prices leading bottle collector Edward Fletcher has devised the following (adjustable) list of bottle ratings:
A: Widespread in dumps of several countries.
B: Widespread in dumps of at least one country.
C: An interesting item, worth collecting, worth buying.
D: A choice collector's piece, difficult to find.
E: Very rare item.
F: Less than 50 examples recorded.

Beer cans

The US produced the first beer can in 1935. Eleven years ago the BCCA—Beer Can Collectors of America—was founded. This year they claim well over 10,000 members world-wide. BCCA's annual "canventions" (sic!) are remarkable for the numbers of collectors defying, with relish, the adage that you can't have your cake and eat it: you can, apparently, have your can and drink its contents. The trick is to pierce it at the base, so leaving the top and any opening device undamaged for posterity.

British cans are highly rated throughout the collecting world. An early gem, and possibly the world's rarest, is the Coronation Brew brought out by H & G Simmonds and dated 1937. A more recent collectable British can is the 2.21 litre party size can that Marks & Spencer, the chain store group, test marketed in the winter of 1975. Because the sales experiment was short lived, and because the beer inside — Ruddles County Ale — is a most drinkable brew, pristine specimens of the M & S can are in short supply.

The original canning problem was perfecting a suitable lining that would protect the beer from the metal. American Can, a company known as CanCo, developed a lining and called it "Keglined". On January 24, 1935, Kreuger's Brewery offered a canned choice of either Kreuger's Finest Beer or Kreuger's Cream Ale. Within five months Kreuger's were taking trade from major US brewers like Anheuser-Busch, Pabst and Schlitz; and they had increased their own production five-fold. By July 1935 a new law decreed that every can of American beer must carry the initials IRTP—Internal Revenue Tax Paid. The law continued in force till 1950, the initials offering the collector a useful aid to dating.

The first cans were flat-top designs. Continental Cans worked out a method of using bottling equipment to make cans. The result—a can that looked like a bottle, became known as a cone top or spout top. An advantage was that it could be sealed, like a bottle, with a crown cap.

The Felinfoel Brewery at Llanelli in Wales produced, in 1936, two sizes of beer can (nine and 12 fluid ounces) either of which are as elixir to the collector today. The war put paid to can production for the domestic market, but canning for the Services went ahead full speed. The "Crowntainer", a 1940 innovation, looked very like the cone top, but it was of two—as opposed to three-piece construction. Perhaps the most collectable crowntainer is the camouflaged version; here the normally cheering colored label became a drab olive - for the sake of a soldier's safety.

The aluminium top, on a steel-bodied can, was an idea of the early Sixties; it was easier to pierce, though a can opener was still needed. Cans with a "lift tab" were introduced in the States in 1962. Odd can openings—there were many experimental types—are now highly rated by beer can collectors. One American can could be opened by using the base of a similar can, which must have encouraged sales.

The can collector looks for all cans brought in "naked" by a small brewing concern to wrap in their own paper labels. Worthington issued a dumpy plastic beer can with a ring pull aluminum top. It looked like an ice cream tub, and was not a great success, but it's worth owning one today. Following the Sixties boom in James Bond movies, an American company launched a series of 007 Special Blend beers, each can featuring a scene of London with a dolly bird in the foreground. Though the beer flopped, the complete series of cans now sells for thousands of dollars.

Nutmeg-graters

Nutmeg appeared in the West in the 12th century. From the start it was seen to be a potent and mysterious drug to cure all ills. In the sick room it was used to fumigate; it sweetened the breath and was even said to ward off the plague. The most common form of nutmeg-grater

Silver nutmeg-graters.

is the pocket or portable one. Nutmeg was added in quantity to many of the hot, warming beverages like posset, caudle, negus, and the more familiar punch and toddy. As well as wines, ales—often far more devastating brews than today's beers—were also mulled. Nutmeg being an expensive spice, the landlord would steady his hand when it came to sprinkling the stuff on—small wonder that the traveling boozer carried his own supply.

The poorer class of imbiber might have a wooden grater - though the item which actually rasped against the nutmeg was made of metal and known as a "rappoir". Wealthier drinkers would have pocket graters made of enamel, silver, ivory and tin. Hand carved graters are known, the cone, nut and egg being common shapes. For those without the necessary skills or patience, the egg-shaped coquillas, a Brazilian palm nut, could be simply polished to bring out the lovely mottled tortoise-shell pattern. Hardwoods, like sycamore, mulberry, and boxwood were also carved. Patterned veneered wood was popular in the early 1800s, when barrel and bottle shapes appeared.

Dating is not too difficult. A favorite 18th century design was that of a heart, hinged to provide access. The rappoir was typically silver up to 1739 (silver continued to be used into the middle of the 19th century), steel up to the 1770s , and tinned rolled steel to the closing years of the century; thereafter blued steel is common. Silver plate is also known, as is japanned tin and engine-turned steel. Sometimes the japanning was done by the lady of the house: magazines showed bored housewives how to do their own Oriental decoration.

Kettles

Originally a kettle was a large cooking pot or cauldron (a usage which lingers in the term fish kettle). The elegant spouted kettle came in with the tea habit, in the 17th century. The earliest known silver kettle is dated 1694. The Dutch were great kettle exporters sending their wares to America and Britain in the 18th century. Althougha particular large kettle is known as a Dutch kettle (it holds about six pints), identifying kettles is a study in itself.

American kettles may feature an unusual flattened or "strap" handle which is attached by hinges fore and aft of the lid. For easy storage, perhaps. Again, the typical goose neck of the American kettle is distinctive, with a squarer bend at the base than English versions. Brass kettles were popular in Britain but elsewhere virtually unknown. Having established a style, a century went by—1750 to 1850

–without a need for change. A peculiarity of Scandinavian kettles is a hinged spout and straight sides. Some American-made kettles bear the maker's name stamped on to the handle. And one craftsman, Kidd of Reading, Pennsylvania, engraved his handles.

Shoddy workmanship in an antique kettle is almost certainly the work of the repairman. The original article would have been meticulously joined, sometimes with a type of dovetailing cut into the metal.

In Britain, Birmingham was the center for brass manufacture. It was hand beaten, cast and die-stamped there from around 1760. The name brass itself has undergone a change over the years. Today it's known as an alloy of zinc and copper. In Elizabethan times what we now call bronze, an alloy of copper and tin, was called brass. Which puts a slightly different complexion on what Shakespeare termed "brazen"!

To keep pace with changing fashions and the importance of tea time, kettles were made together with their own spirit heaters and stands.

A selection of pot-lids and Prattware.

A Martin Hall electroplated tea kettle on lampstand, c. 1875

This meant that tea could be taken by the fire without having to reach into the fire to retrieve the kettle constantly. Spirit heated kettles became known as brown kettles because of a process which colored the base to heatproof it. Where the kettle was of the earlier sort that boiled water from fire heat, there might be a kettle tilter or idleback, a device that hooked around the handle and enabled water to be poured without removing the kettle from its hook over the hearth.

As demand increased lustrous copper and brass gave way to tinplate kettles. The best of these were "block tin", but they were still handmade. Copper bottomed or tinned copper ware was considered best for the iron range of those days.

By the way, if you are feeling pleased with your own copper kettle find, convinced that it has that period look and is suitably burnished and battered from use, remember that there was a vogue for purely decorative fireside metalware at the end of the 19th century.

7

Something To Write Home About

Pens

Writing implements and the paraphernalia of the desk and office—pencil sharpeners, pen knives, desk sets, ink wells, blotters, pen wipers, and a dozen other associated items—have long been within easy reach of the collector on a shoestring budget. The less exciting examples should continue to remain cheap. But the signs are that there will be a stiffening in the prices of such things as glass fountain pens and those decorated in an Art Nouveau or Art Deco style and the early masterpieces of design by current makers like Sheaffer, Waterman's, Mont Blanc, Parker and defunct firms such as Conway Stewart and Swan.

There is already a hankering after the "look" of an old fashioned fountain pen, reflected in the screw cap, chunky shape and bold ball-end clip of the successful Sheaffer No-nonsense range of pens, modeled on an early filling fountain pen in fact. One of the rules of collecting states that where a copy becomes chic the original artifact improves dramatically in value.

An electric typewriter is now as cheap to buy as a good manual machine was a few years ago. The vogue for felt tips and rolling

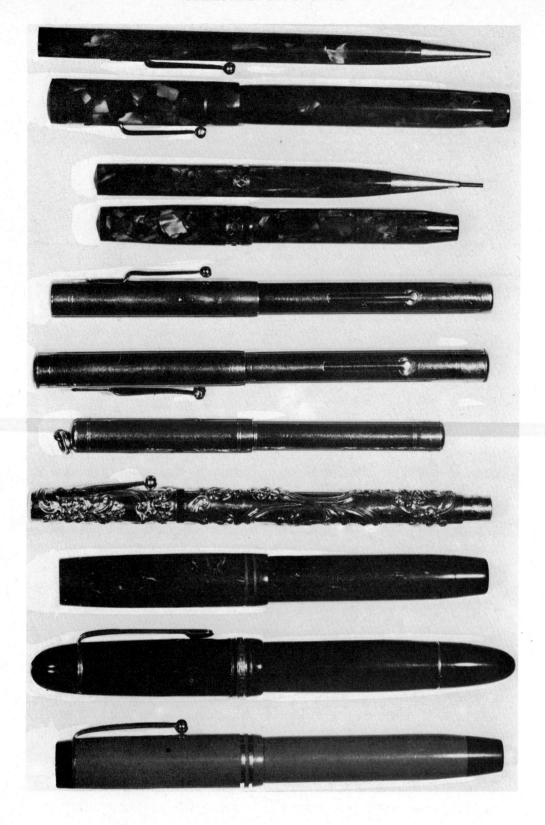

A selection of early pens and mechanical pencils.

markers has further depersonalized handwriting in favor of slickness, speed and reliability. Now there is a hankering after "real" writing, a nostalgic relish for lost caligraphic skills. The mood was confirmed in March 1979 when Christie's in London devoted an entire sale to fountain pens and writing implements consisting largely of the collection of William Bishop, a professional caligrapher who had started collecting as a child. The collection included quill pen cutters, early traveling writing sets, paper knives, pen nib boxes, pen holders, propeling pencils (some disguised as a revolver, pipe, cannon and golf clubs); a walking stick which broke open to reveal a pen, pencil, inkwell—as well as a screw top with a view glass of a nude woman. Two of the rarer items were a pen holder inscribed with the name of Byron's last mistress, Countess Guiccioli, and a silver pen containing, among other things, a spring balance for weighing letters, inscribed John Sheldon 1806, Feb. 8th 1842.

The fountain pens in the sale included Victorian novelty examples and an early glass pen of 1849, an American Art Nouveau style Waterman's "Ideal" pen of black vulcanite with an overlay of pierced white metal, an Art Deco propeling pencil with a perpetual calendar by Tiffany, as well as a selection of early 20th century fountain pens by Mabbie Todd & Co, de la Rue & Co Ltd, and others.

Quill pens (in general use after about 1825) were a bundle of trouble. First there was a shortage of geese to provide suitable feathers. Then the process for turning them into effective writing instruments was complex. The feathers were plunged into hot sand, after which the membrane could be peeled off, the feathers trimmed and the hardened point sharpened, a continuing problem in use. Patent pen knives are a must for a writing collector: look for those where the blade slides out from a hole in the end of the handle; they look a little like a cigar cutter.It has been estimated that in the 1810s the Bank of England was using over a million and a half quill pens a year which meant that each clerk would have used, and jettisoned, five pens a day...

As early as 1809 Bartholomew Folsch had made a pen with an ink reservoir, and a self-supplying quill pen had been produced in 1819. In 1844 a vulcanizing process for rubber offered a material for pen barrels that ink could not corrode.

In 1851, at the Great Exhibition, a certain Mr Cogan demonstrated an all glass pen, with a pointed end and a tiny hole at the tip. The pen sucked up its ink supply by capillary action—but it was probably more trouble than it was worth, thanks to constant blotting.

Steel nibbed pens date from the 1820s; the fountain pen was perfected after 1883 when Lewison Edson Waterman produced his Ideal Safety Pen: at last a pen which would not leak in any but the upright position! Earlier examples had caps designed to plug the flow of ink. The glass reservoir had to be topped up with a filler device like an eye dropper. The side lever which depressed an internal rubber sac was developed around the turn of the century. But even levers failed and some pens had (still have) sacs which are depressed by hand. Unusual filling mechanisms are a worthwhile subsection of fountain pen collecting–the Sheaffer snorkel and self-filling capillary devices and plunger mechanisms are all good finds. The Germans produced a variety of unusual fountain pens, the Schmackelsen, Kollisch, Oidtmann, and Resiert among them.

The manufacture of a fountain pen was a complicated operation involving several hundred steps, a third of them to do with the nib. Once the filling mechanism of a pen was fuss-free, the snob value of a smart outer case could be quickly realized. Splendid examples in gold, silver, rolled gold and engine-turned metal, mother of pearl, lacquer, enamel and wood are all known. Plastic pens in vulcanite, bakelite, etc., are a must for beginners. Named pens, like the Waterman's "New Art" of 1904 and the Parker 5l (designed by Laszlo Moholy-Nagy, the Hungarian artist-designer and associate of Walter Gropius of Bauhaus fame) are all worthy additions to a pen collection. Extra bonus: pens are often easily repaired–and you can use one to impress the bank manager!

Original price tags, publicity material and presentation boxes enhance a collection and its eventual resale value. Association interest can give a dramatic lift to the value of a mundane object like a fountain pen. In March 1979 when Phillips of London auctioned the fountain pen–a Waterman's "Ideal" desk model–used by Edward VIII to sign his abdication (10 December 1936) it sold for £2,000 ($5,000).

Steel nibs and pen holders

It's hard now, looking at my handwriting, to imagine that as a schoolboy I was a champion penman in the Italic style, and actually gave a public exhibition. Perhaps it's the nib I've been using.

Joking apart, anyone who doubts the importance of nibs in writing should talk to a serious collector of just those. The thousands of glittering varieties, the ornate gilding of the packages, the embossing of the nib boxes and cards–there are traveler's sample cards bearing pictures of Napoleon, Nelson and Stephenson's Rocket — have prompted a branch of collecting of their own.

Not only do people still use steel nibs, but there is a continuing demand for the even earlier quill nib. Yet it was the drudgery of preparing, cutting and maintaining in trim the quill nib that led to the introduction of the patent steel nib. Samuel Harrison used tubes of sheet steel with the join forming the slit for the nib in about 1780. Hawkins and Mordan (later famous for propeling pencils) tried horn and tortoiseshell nibs, adding bits of diamonds and ruby to make the tips more resilient.

Doughty's gold nibs were furiously pricey but said to last six years. And Joseph Bramah, wanting the best of both worlds, had patented a machine for cutting quills into economical pieces to stick into pen holders.

The early history of the steel nib was written in Birmingham, England. In 1828 John Mitchell mastered the steel rolling arts which enabled nibs to be machine made. Two years later James Perry devised the hole above the slit which led to a more flexible point. Together with Joseph Gillott (who patented a nib that didn't splay with use) these

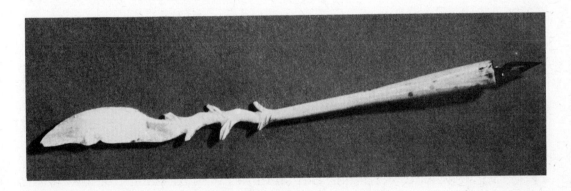

Unusual carved bone pen-holder with letter-opener at the end.

three were the bastion of British — and world — nib making until Camden in New Jersey became the leading manufacturing town after the First World War.

Nib varieties are fun to collect. There's Perry's Regulating Spring Pen of 1843; a sliding spring controlled flexibility. Supposedly non-corrosive Perryian Limpid Ink was another Perry speciality. There were nibs that curved round at an angle, said to be useful for easterners who wrote from right to left, nibs with three points (for ruling cash columns), nibs with five points (for musicians to rule their own manuscript) and a galaxy of ornamental nibs for the stylist and professional caligrapher.

The names of old nibs amuse and amaze today. There was the Welcome Pen No. 1102, the Royal Courts Steel Quill, The Star, the London School Pen, the Time is Money nib which would not "choke splutter or need shaking"—and it had projections under the nib so it could be slipped off and replaced without dirtying fingers. There was the Duke (later the Czarina), the Actuary, the Metallic Quill and the Rob Roy.

Portrait nibs, a European favorite, are highly sought after today. Nibs depicting Queen Victoria, Charles Dickens, Bismarck, Garibaldi, Schiller, and nibs in the shape of the Eiffel Tower, the human hand, and more, are all known.

One of the world's leading dealers, Philip Poole, began collecting 21 years ago when cheap and efficient ball pens (invented in 1937 by Joseph Laszlo Biro, a Hungarian living in Argentina) meant that people were chucking out nibs and he could coax unusual nibs and their gloriously decorated packs, minor masterpieces of display art, from the waste bin.

For the nib collector, pen holders are a must to own. These were stark and utilitarian, ranging from, a pencil-shaped stick with a metal shank and a cork-collared variety, said to cure writer's cramp, to jeweled objets de vertu.

Pen-wipers

The quickest way to ruin an old steel nib was to leave the ink to dry into a crystalline rust-based gunge. Before stainless steel and self drying fountain pens appeared, the pen-wiper was a must for the conscientious writer. Tiny books with cloth pages were sold as little souvenirs and an unmarked one, perhaps with an attractive gold lettered leather cover naming a popular resort, would be a rare find today. Pen-wipers in the shape of a hat—especially a fez—were common. Shot cleaners consisted of a bottle of lead shot. You plunged the nib up and down to remove ink deposits. A sponge, which could be moistened and a short tufted brush were all used and often set into a glass, porcelain, metal or ivory holder elaborately decorated quite beyond its calling.

Pencil holders and propeling pencils

Pencil holders usually look like a slimmer lipstick case. They are frequently gold or silver and may be attached to a chain or bracelet. The pencil stub simply slots in and out on a slide and knob mechanism. The famous William Bishop Collection of writing instruments featured a variety of desirable propeling pencils, like the "WHAT ARE TRUMPS" silver propeling pencil, with a trump indicator for Bridge. Disguised pencils are useful finds. A recently auctioned lot of seven such pencils included one in the shape of a horn, a pipe, a key, an acorn and a letter opener.

There are extending pencils and collapsible pen holders but the most interesting of all are propeling pencils known since the 1822 patent of Samuel Mordan of London. Johann Faber of Nuremberg produced the classic twist-end propeling pencil in 1863. A pencil is a pencil is a pencil apparently to the collector: the real hunt is for propeling pencils that look like a tennis racket, a lady's leg, a toy revolver, stuff like that. And the more additional functions—calculators, rulers, perpetual calendars, bottle openers, letter scales—that the manufacturer could squeeze into the design the better.

Desktop bygones

The centerpiece for a collection of writing memorabilia must be the inkstand, once known as a "standish". Apart from one or two ink containers, one for blue or black ink, one for red—a stand can have a pen holder or tray for pens, a drawer to hold stamps or wafer seals for envelopes, an envelope moistener, a receptacle for clips or pins, a bell to summon one's footman to deliver the letter, a candle sconce to make light of letter writing, and a pounce pot.

The pounce pot is a gem of a find today, and can be mistaken for a pepper pot. It held the sand or cuttlefish powder which was sprinkled on the still wet ink to mop up the surplus moisture. Pounce pots started to get detached from their partners on the writing tray after around 1840 when a Mr Ford discovered blotting paper.

The grandest ink stands are fashioned from ram's or deer heads or the hoof of a much loved but dear departed horse, usually mounted with silver. Lower down the scale would be glass, brass, iron, porcelain, pottery and papier mâché. I bought a crested example of an ink stand recently. It boasts a tray for stamps, a rack for a pen and a lip all the way round at the base to hold pins. A common pewter inkstand features a wide-lipped flanged base, making it almost impossible to topple over; non-spill designs are an interesting sideline in ink bottles and containers. Such stands are still used in some quarters of the British legal profession; lawyers seem to think they help establish an air of timeless authority.

Paper knives

Some metal paper knives, slim and sharp as a rapier, would slit a throat as soon as an envelope. Wooden paper knives come in polished hardwoods, carved ivory, lacquered and decorated in *Chinoiserie;* bronze, pewter, brass, electroplate, gold and silver blades are set into handles of bone, ivory, mother of pearl. Some paper knives are as neat as a fruit knife—yet one in my collection measures 23 inches long. Its brass blade screws into a brass shank set into a great curving antler.Finding out why there are somany materials, shapes and sizes is a real collector's challenge. challenge.

The development of the paper knife is closely connected with postal history. Before 1840, postage rates were calculated on the distance a letter traveled, the number of pieces of paper it contained, and the weight. To save money, the writing paper itself was turned into a do-it-yourself envelope; you simply folded it into three and tucked in the ends. The open flap of such "letter sheets" was sealed with a small sticky disc known as a wafer seal or sealing wax. To remove the seal, a small pointed paper knife was used. A smooth, round handle could be used to make sharp creases along the fold.

Following the invention of patent gum in 1850 the first stick-down envelopes appeared. A slim paper knife with a tapering blade and a sharp edge was needed to slit open the flap.

But what of the baroque monster knife in my collection, and the paper knives that look like canoe paddles (the best of these are carved with oriental landscapes, birds and animals and lacquered)? One explanation is that they were used on parcels and packages. On "THE POPULAR PAPER KNIFE" you can read details of "THE NEW INLAND PARCELS POST" along with a stern warning not to send bladders of liquid, lucifer matches or live animals through the mail! The very slim wood shape, with black spatulate handles, appears to have been a standard pattern which firms had overprinted with their logo or sales message. They date from the late 1800s and the most

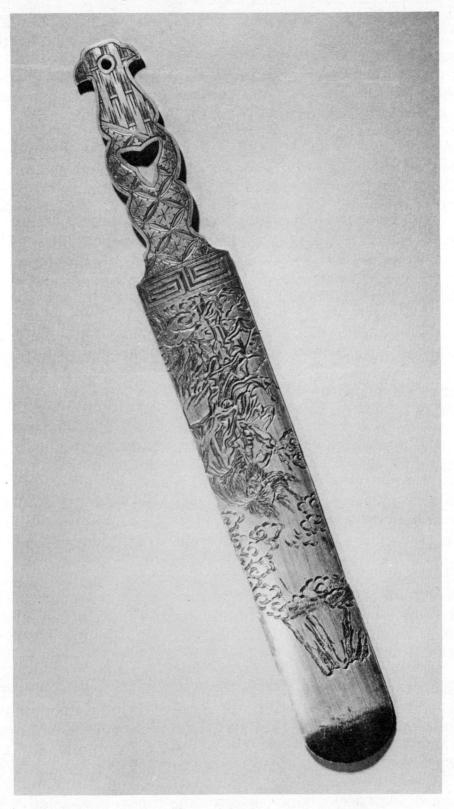

Paperknife.

desirable ones bear a printed date. Some oriental design knives have a hole in the handle for hanging. But why? So you could keep it in handy reach by a favorite reading chair. For the theory is they were used to cut open newspapers. Apparently our ancestors sometimes asked for their newspaper to be delivered uncut round the edges. The idea was to stop servants getting a sneak preview of the news.

Yet another kind of paper knife is associated with books and book-binding. Up to about 1820 books were issued in sheets and bound by the bookseller. A customer could have his pages cut "on the plough". The book was held fast in a vice, spine down, and a plough knife used like a plane, smoothed off the ends into a crescent shape. This would also "open" all the page ends. Or the book buyer could order his book uncut. He would slit each page as he read with a paper knife. Curiously, the rough trimmed edge was considered attractive, and is still a feature of some publishers' wares.

Some book knives come with a section of the small blade cut out, to make a kind of tongue or flap. The knife was slipped over the page like a big paper clip, to keep the place. A favorite 19th century pattern had a handle of semi-precious stone with a blade of silver in the shape of a bricklayer's trowel. These can cost up to about $50 (£20).

I prefer to collect interesting knives rather than precious ones, though they do exist. Fin de siècle knives can be found with repoussé silver handles and elegant ivory blades. But you can pick up the treen variety (hand carved wood) for only a couple of dollars in a bric-à-brac store - if you keep your eyes open. I have one with a crisply carved Edelweiss bouquet as the handle; another, oak, features acorns in the carved design. A more important find was a knife carved in the shape of a violin neck. Possibly it had once been part of a real miniature violin made for a child, but had got broken. Or the knife may have been the work of an apprentice violin maker, his little tour de force showing his master he'd learned his craft and was now ready to tackle the real thing.

Souvenir knives are well collected: some have little peepholes in the handle: look through, against the light, for a diminutive photographic view of a seaside resort. Inscriptions and endearments add interest too. I have a knife perhaps made by a convict or homesick sailor with the word "MOM" intricately fretted out of the wood.

The most expensive paper knives are those associated with a celebrity. Benjamin Disraeli, one of the most colorful British political figures of the 19th century, kept a 14-inch long paper knife on his writing table in his study at Hughendon, in Buckinghamshire. Christie's expected it to make up to £100 in February 1978; instead it was knocked down at £550 ($1,200).

Blotters and blotter-holders

The typical blotter has a curved underside, usually wood, around which the blotting paper was wrapped. The top section is rectangular with a buttonlike handle to grip. You rocked it gently over the writing. The decoration, and value, in a blotter is expressed in the ornamentation of the top and the handle, which can be papier mâché, brass, copper, pinchbeck, repoussé worked silver, or inlaid with mother of pearl. Handsomely carved treen (wood) examples are also worth buying and often the cheapest. If your ship comes in you may discover a blotter with a compartment designed to hold postage stamps and a mint condition old stamp still in it.

Blotter holders are large flat usually leather-bound boards into which a sheet of blotting paper can be slipped. The tooling of the leather provides the collecting interest although some have silver mounts to hold the paper in at the corners.

Typewriters

Still serviceable old typewriters get discarded for reasons of fashion, which is bad business sense but good news for collectors who can often pick up important early machines at bargain basement prices. I have a hunch that women may soon be joining the collecting ranks - for sentimental reasons. The typewriter played a vital part in emancipation. Being a typist in the late 19th century was a respectable occupation. It meant that a girl could venture alone among men, without her chaperone, for the very first time!

Mark Twain described his early typewriter as this "curiosity breeding little joker". He is said to have submitted the first typed manuscript to a publisher — his *Life on the Mississippi*. But he had a curious love/hate relationship with the new-fangled contraption, concluding that a typewriter was fine for work (though his wrote only in capitals), but not suitable for private correspondence. Every time he sent out a typed letter he had to send another to explain to the amazed recipient how he'd done it.

It was precisely to save time – especially in business – that spurred on "the father of the typewriter", Christopher Latham Sholes. Others had produced ingenious devices that would tap out a neat line of print. But their typewriters had no speed advantage over handwriting. Marseilles printer Xavier Progin discovered that it was best to have type on individual bars, arranged in a circle, and striking at the same point - just as on modern machines. Guiseppe Ravizza was probably the first to use an inked ribbon. Charles Thurber had his letters fixed to peculiar plungers: typing was rather like playing the trumpet. He also devised the roller-platen which moved along, carrying the paper, another essential ingredient of the successful typewriter.

Eventually, Sholes correlated the lessons of these individuals and between 1867 and 1869 produced 30 prototypes before he made a machine that would outpace pen and ink. The first practical machine was patented in 1868 by Sholes and Carlos Glidden of Milwaukee. It sat on top of a sewing machine chassis and the operator had to depress a foot pedal to turn up each line. In 1873 Sholes and his associate signed up with E. Remington, then a maker of guns and sewing machines: the typewriter industry was born.

In 1885 a bizarre battle took place between Sholes and his followers and the inventors of the Caligraph. Which machine was faster? That was the question. Sholes had pioneered the QWERTY arrangement of keys because it enabled fast typing without jamming them up. McGurrin was the touch-typing wizard on a Sholes machine.

The Caligraph, on the other hand, had an astonishing 72 keys—one each for signs, numerals, capitals and lower case — arranged in alphabetical order. The Caligraph also had a champion, a two-finger tapper by the name of Traub. Traub needed to study the keyboard as he typed, but was convinced he could thrash McGurrin.

The build-up to this typing "duel" was the 1888 equivalent of a Muhammad Ali fight. Needless to say, McGurrin won—hands down. After the fiasco—not surprisingly—no-one wanted to buy Caligraphs, and the firm went out of business. Today, however, Caligraphs are highly collectable. The earliest ones have a distinctive platen: instead of being round and smooth, it is slightly faceted along its length, to correspond to the lines of type. Blickensderfer is another famous name typewriter. The aluminium "Featherweight" of 1893 was the first portable and years ahead of its time in design. It used the type-wheel principle. Instead of being attached to rods, the type is set into a metal wheel that revolves as the keys are struck, to present the right letter. It was a forerunner of the "golf ball" system. By simply changing the

ball or wheel you have a whole new alphabet at your fingertips. A Blickensderfer No. 5 Manual can be picked up for around $80 (£30).

One primitive early typewriter that could start a collection is the Lambert. It features a circular dial, rather like a telephone, with letters instead of numbers. You select the letter you require, one at a time, and give the dial a meaningful clump. It is about as speedy as today's labelmaking machine, but one of many milestones along the way to today's word processor.

If you know of a firm which is going out of business or about to be given a face-lift get friendly with the doorman or janitor. Interesting early machines, destined for the trash can, could be yours for the price of a drink. Old office equipment is often auctioned as a job lot, and early typewriters are often included. A shop that repairs typewriters may have ancient trade-ins or unclaimed repairs. Asking costs nothing.

Lilian Sholes at one of her father's experimental typewriters, 1872.

P.S. Writing sets for desk top or traveling, writing compendiums and traveling inkstands are all "musts" for the collector of writing paraphernalia, as are writing slopes, often inlaid with elaborately tooled leather but probably minus the glass inkwell. Springloaded secret compartments may yield an old gold cufflink or a rare stamp, though more often an old marble or photo.

A paper-clip, now a boring piece of wire, was once a giant size springloaded device of clam-like tenacity. Look for elaborate die stamped patterns picked out in gold and bright enamel, those in the shape of horse shoes, clam halves or a pair of hands (the silver version is particularly attractive). Consider also pencil sharpeners and drawing instruments for draughtsman or artist, like the 19th century Pantograph, a wooden device like a piece of garden trellis which enabled drawings to be copied and scaled down or up merely by following the original outline.

8

Rock Back The Clock

Don't knock Rock. That's the message going out to collectors with a musical bent. Today Rock is rapidly acquiring its own collecting clique whose "spoils" embrace musical instruments (not all of them modern), and the quintessentially 20th century ephemera—like badges, plastic busts of the stars, printed T-shirts, song sheets, programs, posters, fan club missives, concert tickets, records and record sleeves.

The musical instruments represent the top end of the range to the collector, not least because many of them, like the guitars dating back to the Sixties made by prestige American firms like Gibson, Martin, and Fender are, notwithstanding the pioneering patina, legacy of a thousand hectic "live" performances, *still* the best instruments to play.

Guitars

Martin guitars are recognized as being among the finest popular music instruments ever produced. Particular years produced vintage models and people collect old Martins and "lay them down" like fine wine to accrue in value. At first sight a Martin looks not unlike the docile classical or Spanish guitar. But it is a different beast. Made mostly by hand—as they have been since the end of the 18th century—a Martin features six or

12 metal strings and internal bracings to take the greater strain than is exerted on a nylon-strung classical guitar. A Martin is also usually an acoustic, i.e. a non-electric guitar, but it is still associated with some of the biggest names in Rock, country music and folk, people like Bob Dylan, Steve Stills, Joan Baez, Hank Snow, Hank Williams, and Gene Autrey and Johnny Cash. (To make it sound louder, an acoustic guitar is simply played close up to one or more microphones.)

The Martin family began guitar making in Markneukirchen in Saxony. When the local violin-makers took offense at the cabinet-making Martin family turning their hand to guitar manufacture, previously an exclusive province to a violin maker, George Frederick Martin sailed for New York. That was in 1833. In the early days, Martin's market areas used to be New York. Then Martin guitars began to spread over the land tracing the expansion of the country westward, across the Oregon mountains, into Pittsburg, down the Ohio river and the Mississippi and into New Orleans. If pioneering settlers, headed west, were of a musical disposition, and their covered wagons concealed a guitar, then that guitar would very likely be a Martin. Needless to say, the dedicated detective collector will see here a clue to research which could well lead to uncovering some of the earliest Martins.

Martins are known by their numbers. The rarest of all is the style 34, similar to the 30 which is in its turn similar to the model 28. Early 28s had herringbone marquetry around the top or sound board. The 30 had inlaid abalone (mother of pearl) around the sound hole and colored wood inlay around the top. The 34 differs in that it features an ivory bridge. A 34 sold today would yield a retirement income. Dating of the earliest Martins is tricky; one model believed to date to 1830 has a modern-looking machine head, with the tuning pegs down one side. The label inside reads: "C. Frederick Martin, Guitar and Violin Manufacturer, Importer of Musical Instruments, Hudson Street, New York." From 1839 to 1867 the labels read: C.F. Martin, New York." And from 1867 until 1898, "C.F. Martin & Son, New York." All Martin guitars were stamped "New York" because an agency operated from there. In 1898, however, the endorsement was changed to Nazareth, Pa., no doubt as an acknowledgement that the country was growing up and that anything outside the main city centers was not necessarily Hicksville.

Another dating clue lies in the finish. Shellac was used between 1833 and 1909, varnish up to 1933 and lacquer thereafter. Although Martins are, pricewise, out of range of this book, the styling is so restrained, the appearance of even a fairly new model so subdued (on many, though not all, Martin models), that they can be overlooked and bargain finds are possible – if you know what to look for. I say this in the light of bitter personal experience.

One of Martin's rare failures could turn out to be a success story for a guitar collector who's done his homework. Because Martin were heavily into the country and folk music area they styled a new model electric guitar on a rival instrument put out by the Gretsch firm, known as the Chet Atkins model. The GT70 and GT75 Martins gleamed like new car bumpers; they came in "deep polished burgundy or black" with "lustrous white pickguards". But it was a stunning sound, not sensational looks that players wanted, and the firm admits that the pickups (microphones under the strings) were not the best. However, some good came from the experiment. Martin produced an SS-140 amplifier to partner their electric guitars. The amp, with solid state circuitry and twin 15 inch Lansing speakers is still lauded, played and it is bound to be collected.

Banjos

American minstrel troupes got the banjo bandwagon started in around 1843. Today early banjos are catching on, and some grab the imagination as well as the ear. The 1840 "tack head" banjo used upholstery tacks to hold the vellum or drumskin in place over the wooden hoop. This primitive tuning technique guaranteed "hot music", because to tighten the vellum and give it resonance, the player had to heat his instrument in front of a fire.

Serious collectors aspire to own banjos made before 1900. As a rough guide to age, banjos with six or seven strings are likely to date before the turn of the century. Latterday banjos have, typically, four or five strings. The rarest early banjo of all is a nine-stringer. Fretless necks are another pointer to an early date. The frets are the strips of brass or nickel silver that graduate the neck and mark out the notes. Yesterday's banjoist had to make do with a fingerboard as smooth as that of a violin and learn the notes by rule of thumb. If the strings are tightened by violin-type push-in pegs this may also indicate a 19th century banjo; patent non-slip pegs came later. A closed-in back, a feature that did not really catch on before 1860-1870, is also a helpful dating clue. W. Temlett introduced his patent closed-back banjo in 1869 and dubbed himself the pioneer of the zither-banjo, so called because of its steel strings and unusual stringing arrangement, whereby the fifth string is carried from the peg under the fingerboard

*Reuben E. Reubens with a few of the banjos in his
extraordinary collection.*

in a tube to reappear at the fifth fret. Traditionally the banjo has a
further tuning peg inserted behind that fret, screwing into the arm at
right angles and parallel to the fingerboard.

Two Americans are to thank for the further development of the zither-banjo. C.E. Dobson patented an "Improved Closed Back" in 1878, and Alfred D. Cammeyer introduced the zither-banjo to Britain in 1888. Cammeyer, a native of New York, produced some of the finest banjos ever seen, notably the Super Vibrante model which boasts exceptionally fine mother of pearl inlay on the peghead and fingerboard. A rare Cammeyer, known as the Colonial, was designed for export to the British colonies; it featured nickel silver banding around the top and bottom of the outer hoop as a deterrent to termites. The finger-board was screwed in place as well as glued to stop warping in exceptional humidity.

Minstrels grew fond of their banjos and loved to decorate them. One collector who specializes in pre-1900 banjos has a Tunbridgeware model on which the vellum is inscribed with names of popular old songs, such as "Down by the Riverside" and "Silver Moon". One of his prize specimens is a banjo picked up in France. Its c.1890 owner was more than a player, he was an artist as well and used the stretched skin as a canvas. On it he painted a striking naval battle in oils. As a banjo it was dear at $250 (£100); but as a fine seascape it was a bargain. Another banjo is made entirely of whale bone.

Banjos built between this century's Great Wars have also a particularly fine pedigree. Many of the most sought after instruments were made by men who were themselves players — among them Stewart and Van Eps in the US and Temlett, Tilley, Dallas and Spencer in Britain. Celebrated soloists like Cammeyer had his designs executed by master craftsman Sydney Young and banjo virtuoso Tarrant Bailey Jr. directed Abbott to carry out his specifications.

When considering a purchase, check the "action" (unless your interest in the instrument is purely decorative). The action – how easy it is to press the strings to the fretboard and "finger" chords all the way up to the highest register—should be comfortable. Otherwise your fingertips will suffer until they become calloused. Action can sometimes be lowered, but only by experienced players or repairmen. Sight along the neck, with one eye closed, as you would along the barrel of a rifle. First "aim" from the peghead towards the body, then from the tail towards the peghead. Check for warps and dips in the fingerboard. But do not mistake for a blemish the intentional dip on the twelfth fret of a banjo. Play a few notes and listen for buzzes and other extraneous noises. These may indicate loose tuning rollers, buttons or pegs (not serious), sprung frets (displaced frets are replaceable) or loose struts, etc., within the body (more serious). When buying any old fretted instrument, go with someone who is knowledgeable, and when in doubt, don't pay out.

Most banjos, being fairly low priced items, don't reach the major auction houses; instead they sell through ads in the classified columns of music papers, in general trading magazines or in music shops.

Unusual 6-string banjo made by W. Ryan in about 1845.
The vellum is tinted green.

Record sleeves

After about 1910 records were sold in paper envelopes, though all the information went on the label in the center of the disc. It wasn't record companies who started decorating the cover, it was the record shops. The album idea came in long before it was technically possible to have a long-playing disc. The first albums of around 1920 were "books" made up of classical recordings in most cases. The modern LP cover as a conscious and collectable art form began with the Beatles and has been gaining momentum ever since. Now record covers have become icons of the Sixties and Seventies, providing instant recognition that has not only boosted sales, but has also done much to improve the quality of contemporary illustration. Some LP covers are landmarks in graphic design and are as sought-after as the fashion plates and music cover of the Deco and Art Nouveau eras. The original artwork that provided the illustration for printing is also rapidly becoming a collectable commodity.

Record cover design by Patrick Woodroffe.

Sometimes, of course, the designers tried too hard. Andy Warhol specified a real miniature zip in the jeans picture that embellished the cover of the Rolling Stones' album, "Sticky Fingers". In a typically bizarre Warhol happening, millions of records were damaged in transit. For the Small Faces' record, "Ogden's Nut Gone Flake", instead of the usual 12" x 12" square sleeve, a circular folder, in the shape of a tobacco tin, was used. The discs kept rolling off the shelves in the record shops. Pop era artists Peter Blake and Richard Hamilton designed the Beatles' albums "Sergeant Pepper's Lonely Hearts' Club Band" and "The White Double Album", respectively. Sometimes even the performers got in on the illustration act. Bob Dylan, Joni Mitchell and Cat Stevens have all, rather optimistically perhaps, had a go. Dylan's self-portrait showed that his pen is mightier than his paintbrush; and Joni Mitchell's self-portrait cover on the LP "Clouds", although technically accomplished, has a prettiness that sits uneasily with some of the songs.

Sleevophiles with a leaning towards jazz will find collectable covers from much earlier. Warhol was designing album covers long before he became a force on the art scene; his designs for guitarist Kenny Burrell's albums "Kenny Burrell" and "Blue Lights" (Liberty Records) mimic the style of Japanese woodblock artist Sugimura.

The trappings of Rock

If you don't believe that Rock is collectable, know that London's Victoria and Albert Museum's Theater Museum, under the curatorship of Alexander Schouvaloff, has been acquiring Rock relics with unusual gusto. They already have a pale grey worsted jacket with velvet collar and box-pleated back owned by Ringo Starr (the Beatles drummer, in case you don't remember), plus Ringo's collarless jacket, in the military style that became the Beatles' trademark. There's a jacket made out of flags – the red lions of Scotland at the rear, the yellow English lions in the front – sometime property of The Who's John Entwistle; an Elton John stage outfit complete with multi-colored lurex stripes, mud-guards on the shoulders and rhinestone-studded platform-soled boots.

In March 1980, Sotheby's sold a paper napkin for £500 ($1,250): it bore a smudgy autograph of Elvis Presley and had come from the Las Vegas Riviera Hotel, scene of one of The King's last perfomances. The same sale saw 14 early photographs of the Beatles sell for nearly twice the pre-sale estimate; four dollar bills signed by the mop-haired Liverpool lads were snapped up by an eager collector. Following the sale the auctioneer commented: "In view of the response we will probably consider holding some more auctions of Rock memorabilia."

The irony is that pop stars, rich beyond the dreams of Croesus in their lifetimes, can actually be worth more dead (Elvis's estate has, since his death, netted well over $1,200 million). Elvis fans make pilgrimages to his grave at Gracelands, buy his records, reissued by the lorryload, watch old Elvis movies, and invest in chunks of his old cars; Elvis's books go for up to $120 each and a Presley Bible sold for $2,000. Before Elvis signed with RCA he made five singles; these now sell for close on $500, and the record sleeves, so often thrown away, are worth even more.

Magazines about the Beatles and Rolling Stones and "The Beatles Monthly", a fan club publication that was produced in the mid-Sixties and ran for about seven years, are selling for $2.50 (£1) a copy. Beatle guitar-shaped pins, brooches, drinks coasters, diaries sell well. Beatle souvenir tablecloths fetch a handy price, as do Beatle handkerchiefs, fan club discs with the group's Christmas message, and the Beatles tin tray (featured on one of their album covers). The song "Yellow Submarine" inspired a number of suitably shaped and colored mementoes. Most coveted of all Beatle items, apart from first editions of John Lennon's two books or a cancelled Beatles passport, is the US album sleeve which shows the four lads dressed up as butchers packing baby dolls; it was too bloody, said the authorities, who banned it. Now the cover alone, even without the disc, can command $250.

Photo of Elvis inscribed by him, which was auctioned at Sotheby's.

9

Oddments

To round off, I've gathered some of the oddments of collecting: fascinating little pieces that fall under the fingers of a collector as he goes about his main collecting preoccupation, or items that do not really fit into any of the earlier chapters of this book yet rate more than a passing mention.

Marbles

If collecting marbles was good enough for George Washington, Thomas Jefferson and John Adams, then could it be the making of you, too?

"Small bowls" was the name of the game in those days, and all three men were classy players. I remember having hundreds of marbles as a child, most of them about three quarters of an inch across, made of clear glass with a swirl of colored glass inside looking somewhat like a contorted sting ray trapped in an ice ball. But I never did know what to do with them as far as the game went. If I had those marbles today I'd sure know what to do with them: keep them safe. Then I'd try to add some of the gems of the hobby, like the pottery and stone marbles and the superb glass specimens, like the swirls and the sulphides. Curiously, the one material that appears rarely to have been turned into a marble is marble itself.

Rare sulphides can cost from $50 (£20) and more. Metal figures of angels, animals, birds and fish were set into heated glass; they can be up to two inches across, and sometimes the figure ended up skewiff. The pre-1900 handmade German marbles are the best to own, although sulphides were made in the US in the 1900s. The swirls, with their colors entwined like streamers from a maypole—used a technique that was to yield the glass paperweights of the 19th century. Colored glass canes, already twisted, were imprisoned in a spherical glass ball by placing them in a two-part mold. The covering glass may be clear or tinted blue or green. Crystal clear glass can indicate a modern version, as old marbles almost always have some discoloration.

If you come across a marble holder at a garage sale, a shallow wooden dish like a polished breadboard with half round holes for retaining the marbles, keep looking for the marbles that fitted it: the Benningtons, spatters, crockery, clay, jade, onyx, carnelian and jasper marbles may not be far behind!

Marbles were at their peak of popularity in the mid 19th century; big marbles measuring perhaps two inches across were named "bouncers", though swirls are known as massive as eight inches in diameter.

One of the curiosities of the game of marbles is that the playing items themselves, the marbles, are at risk and change hands with a win. The player who fancies his chances will risk an important "alley" as many a 19th century boy called his important marbles; another youth, lacking in courage, might venture only a mean "taw" as the lesser balls were known (and also the game). A "commoney" was another type of taw. In *Bardell v Pickwick* (the legal wrangle of *The Pickwick Papers*), Mr Sergeant Buzfuz refers to alley taws or commoneys; he took them to be "a particular species of marbles much prized by the youth of this town."

A cheap substitution for buying marbles was to crack open a Codd stoppered bottle to extract the glass marble which provided an air-tight seal and kept in the mineral water's fizz. Stones placed in a tumbling machine were another way of obtaining workmanlike marbles at next to no charge. (If you come across a bubbly bit of green glass that looks like a flattened marble with its base lopped off, that isn't a marble, but a Victorian doorstop.)

Marble making goes back to the Romans and was revived by the Venetians in about the 14th century. Bohemia and Silesia were on the marble route a hundred years later and the Low Countries, France and England got the habit afterwards. Slate from Coburg in Germany was made into balls nicknamed Dutch (corruption of "Deutsch") stonies. Plain pottery marbles became "taws" or "alley taws"; "blood alleys" were streaked with red. Black and white glazed pottery marbles earned the sobriquet Chinamen. Steel balls had a showing at the beginning of this century, especially in Pennsylvania and Connecticut, but they lacked the charm of glass and pottery.

Connecticut has remained a focal point for marble collectors to this day: write the Marble Collectors Society of American, PO Box 222, Trumbull, Connecticut 06611 about their quarterly newsletter. The best book to read is *Collecting Antique Marbles* by Paul Baumann.

Pincushion ladies

These are the miniature porcelain busts or torsos usually no more than a couple of inches high, that were sewn to little skirts, which covered a useful pincushion. You can recognize pincushion ladies by the holes in the base to which the skirt would have been stitched. As well as pincushions, the models, attached to a filmy type of skirt, were used as lamp shades: in the early days of electric light the harsh glare upset some. Women's magazines of the day also suggested that the skirts could be used as secret stores for a mirror and a powder puff - if they were tucked in the doll's baggy bloomers!

The ladies date from the early 1900s to about the 1930s. The early figures show that period's taste for big, busty women with bold coloring and flowing dresses, often blonde or brown. Some came bald but mohair wigs were available for the seamstress who fancied herself as a hairdresser. The makers of play-doll heads in Thuringia and Bavaria quickly appreciated the sophisticated adult market for detailed small-scale heads as used on pincushion ladies. The most desirable models are those which display an imaginative arrangement of the arms, since it was more difficult to create models with arms held away from the body. Individual fingers and elegant wrists are a further sign of quality. Eventually the arms became separate, jointed items.

Some of the models are numbered underneath; others have marks and letters to indicate the makers. Galuba and Hoffman of Ilmenau and Dressel Kister of Passau are two of the greatest makers' names to note. The Passau factory's mark is a reversed blue question mark. Stroebel & Wilken, another company, often have "S & W" plus a number on the base.

19th century bark mask from British Columbia.

Dating is easiest when the models are dressed in contemporary clothing styles; cloche hats, long beads, flat-chested dresses, neck-ties, and so on. Any pincushion lady with a distinctly Egyptian look grafted on to a typically European lady's face can be accurately pin-pointed to 1922: that was the year Tutankhamun's tomb was opened and the country went wild for Egyptiana. A pincushion lady dressed and coiffed in an 18th century style is not contemporary, but merely an example of a fad from the Deco years.

Masks

African masks are among the most striking. Normally they are of carved wood or ivory and were used for war, by medicine men, or in dances. Animal masks had a special significance: the natives believed that the qualities of the beast, like the strength and bravery of a lion, would be magically transferred to the wearer. Quite recently a fine collection of African art including a tribal funerary mask was sold in Manchester, England. The owner's husband had formed the collection during the late 1920s when he was employed as a representative for a wood merchant company. The mask had come from the Ogowe River area of the south-west Gabon. It had all the characteristics for which carvings of that area have become famous - the slanted slit eyes, the kaolin wash, the triangular chignon hair style. These are the features which the M'Pongwe tribe believed would invoke the spirit of the dead. It sold for £2,400 ($6,000). An unusual softwood mask carved with three faces with kaolin wash over a black painted ground fetched £300 ($750); and a white-faced funerary mask with scarification marks and black painted lips went for £350 ($850).

The American Indian also produced a variety of ceremonial masks, from those that completely enveloped the head to masks that merely hid the front of the face. In the south-western part of South America the natives favored a cylindrical mask. In religious tribal dances masks were carried on long poles which were then placed in front of dwellings. A collector who specializes in Wild West memorabilia tells me that American Indians are to this day so moved by the powerful medicine imbued in their ancient ritual masks that they revere them almost as living gods and travel to museums where the masks are exhibited for a ceremonial "feeding of the faces".

Spectacles

There is a glimmering of interest in yesterday's spectacles and eye-glasses. The trouble with the earliest spectacles was that no one knew how to keep them in place. The Orientals used bands going over the head and under the ears; or cords, with weights attached, were fastened to the lenses, passed over the ears, so the weights hung down over the chest. In the early days of the pince-nez idea, spectacles that gripped the bridge of the nose, the belt and braces principle was employed: supportive cords also went round the ears. "Temple spectacles" did not appear probably before 1727, when Edward Scarlett of London fashioned the first frame to have rigid side pieces and curved ends to rest on the ears. Some of the oddest shaped early frames have splayed side pieces so they could sit, not on the ears, but on the wings of a wig. Monocles became popular soon after. Lorgnettes—glasses on a stick—quizzers, spy glasses and lens-triers (early sight-testing gadgets), are also worth a place in a spectacle collection, as are early bi-focals:Benjamin Franklin sported one of the earliest pairs of bi-focals in around 1760. In the late 19th century it was possible to purchase optical goods by mail order. Montgomery Ward, the Chicago firm,issued a catalog in 1895 which included a do-it-yourself sight-testing chart.

Easiest to find—and buy—are old iron-framed glasses, followed by steel, nickel and gold. Cased folding-frame spectacles are a rare find, as are glasses with frames that match their case. Inside 19th century and early 20th century cases look for engraved advertising blurbs of the opticians.

Horse furniture

Riding tackle was made to be used, and after a hard day's ride the groom lavished time and energy to keep the leather gleaming and the metal parts bright. Today's collector of horse "furniture" treasures rosettes, bits, harness, spurs and stirrups and, of course, horse brasses. Horse brasses were originally employed as amulets, some say, to ward off the "evil eye" as well as the flies. Brasses from the 1700s were simply flat discs, known as sunflashes, because they reflected the heat of the sun, keeping it off the horse's head.

After the Napoleonic wars, brasses were made in the shapes of bells, lions, thistles. Railway companies depicted their locomotives; famous people appeared and important events were commemorated.

True early horse brasses are a rare find; nor are they cheap. Don't be taken in by the modern, rough-cast versions in the gift shops. Handle a late 18th or 19th century brass to get the feel of the real thing. They were cut from the sheet or cast from quality metal, worked by hand

and deeply burnished both by the original craftsman and by the user. Handpolishing over the years will have given the metal a silky sheen which cannot be reproduced, even though many have tried to fake early horse brasses. The chafe marks of the leather harness against the brass are also impossible to reproduce and can be easily spotted by the collector who knows what he is about. To save continual cleaning brasses can be painted over with a light, clear varnish and they will never lose their lustre.

A more modest collector's start can be made with horse rosettes. These can be picked up at country auctions very cheaply. Rosettes go at the corner of the bridle on harness horses and stallions being led in a parade. Steel, brass or plated, they look like oversized medallions and often bear elaborate monograms or attractive coats of arms: a little research in a book of genealogy can help date your find and identify the former owner.

Bits are a newer area for collectors. Being made of iron, until the introduction of stainless steel around the time of the First World War, they need special attention to protect them from rust. A lorimer (maker of horse furniture) told me that the groom would rub away at the bit, using silver sand and a burnisher so they would come up as shiny as chromium plate. The stable was kept warm, too, to keep out the damp. The chain mail epaulette worn by the Yeomanry originated from the need to burnish bits. Because they are so often tarnished, cast iron bits are often knocked down at country auctions at silly prices. But cleaned up they look a treat. Snaffle bits are the simple ones; they work on the corner of the horse's mouth usually. The Pelham bit might press on the beast's tongue as well, ensuring a quick response to the rider's wishes. And there are many unusual bits of patent design, mostly 19th century, waiting to be discovered.

Picture frames

The first pictures were religious; church paintings were framed to look as if they were housed in their own little archway or temple with a pointed roof. In the 12th and 13th centuries simple wood frames appeared. These were often colored or engraved. Some of the oldest Italian frames feature a stipple effect. A punch was used to create whirls and lines. Very bold, chunky carving in the wood may be baroque Spanish work. Curiously, the earlier the frame the easier it is to pin-point its country of origin, because people, and their ideas, traveled less before the Renaissance. King Francis 1 of France (1494-1547) invited numbers of Italian wood carvers to his country and they

16th century picture frame.

developed a style now held to be typically French, which includes leaf, "egg and dart", and ribbon carving. The best ribbon work rises high off the wood of the frame and looks just like silk caught on a breeze. France led the world in picture framing in the 17th and 18th centuries. Frames made in the reign of Louis XV are heavy with carved fruit. But by Louis XVl's time the extroverted look was out: instead neat beading and delicate filigree work was all the rage. The French preferred oak; or they used a softwood facing on an oak backing. The Italians favored soft fruitwood—which explains why Italian frames are so often riddled with worm.

After carving, wood would be treated with gesso, another name for plaster of Paris. Then the gilder would sharpen up the edges of the whitened carving and on went a special glue size, followed by gold leaf. The Dutch preferred natural wood in its dark and lustrous shades, especially walnut, fruitwood, oak and ebony, which were all available to them because of their strong trading links with the Far East.

Few frames are signed. And dating is difficult; the true guide to a frame's quality and age is, oddly enough, on the back. Study the corner joins first. If there is a wedge-shaped piece of wood across the corner, at right angles to the mitre line, the frame is probably French or English. These two countries also pinned their corners with wooden dowel, through the "elbow" of the join. If the wood at the corner overlaps this could indicate an Italian origin. In the early days nails were unknown. Until the 19th century all nails were forged by hand, individually. Later they were stamped out of flat sheets of iron and you can tell these by their square edges and tapering shanks. Most recent nails are made of wire; these have a round or oval cross-section. It used to be possible to pick up picture frames for a song in the corners of back rooms and junk shops. Now they are collected in their own right and sometimes hoarded to await the time when a suitably sized picture falls into the hands of the collector.

"Jumpers"

Old Dutch tiles have lost popularity as collectables today. But there is an area which can be thoroughly, and profitably, explored. Many of the finest 17th century tiles have a static quality about them, but not all. The "jumpers" are the exception; they show animals on the point of leaping up. It might be a dog, a horse with rider or a rabbit. Early jumpers have the animal's hind legs still on the ground, roughly shown by a few blades of grass sketched in with swift, deft strokes. Later examples leave out the foliage; instead, a little shadow beneath the animated creature gives a similar effect, as well as enhancing the feeling of depth. The more color there is the better, as the blue on white background tiles are more common.

Spanish copy of a Dutch "Jumper".

Door furniture

Knockers, door bells, hinges, door handles, knobs, letter-box flaps, keys, brass and porcelain finger-plates (to keep muddy marks off the wooden sides of a door) all qualify as door furniture. Turned wooden door knobs are most common; white metal, brass and bronze knobs follow; rare decorated porcelain knobs date from the late 18th century.

Door knockers began to be popular about the time of the late 16th century. Brass, iron and gunmetal—stamped, pierced, wrought or engraved—were common. Look for novelty door knockers, often heavily cast, in the shape of animals' feet, human hands or the head of a lion. The ring through the lion's mouth is the hammer part. If he has pierced eyes it was to enable the person answering the door to size up the caller first and open only if it was a welcome visitor.

Door bells came in in the 19th century. The first were simple bell pulls that jangled an actual thistle-shaped bell suspended in the house or alongside the door. Bells that rang with a sliding mechanism followed. In the 1880s the rotary bell appeared: the caller turned a key on the outside of the door to operate the bell which was fixed inside. I have not come across faked bells but there has been a lot of very good forgery in knockers and letter flaps. A truly old letter-box flap shows signs of wear in the screws that attached it to the door; crooks generally stick to faking the front only.

Corner furniture

Even a person who lives in the tiniest home has room for a piece of furniture that fits in the corner of a room–or so you'd think. Sadly, this isn't always so. I can vouch for how hard it is to find a free corner in a modern home. The windows take up too much room, the heating butts into the corners or the doors are too close for comfort. In happy expectation of a move to a more appropriate dwelling, I am on the lookout for corner chairs, corner tables, corner commodes and corner cupboards (hanging and standing).

Corner chairs are the most common. A delight to look at is the style with the captain's style chair back, with out-turned elbow rests and a curved, carved backrest of ample proportions. The best 18th century ones have a cabriole leg at the front in the center, plain legs at the side (against the wall) and one leg at the back (in the point of the corner). Corner chairs look fine but feel as if you are straddling a horse when you try to sit in them in the ordinary way. The answer is to sit in them sideways, so the squab of the seat is against your derrière in the normal way, not with the pointed part between your legs. Then you have a back support and an arm to lean on. So are the other arm and

Double arm decorator lamp.

half back redundant? Not at all. So the story goes, these are lovers' chairs: the young man sits sideways on and his lady sits on his lap resting her back and arm against the other half. No wonder some people call corner chairs roundabout chairs! You'll find them in oak, elm, mahogany and fruitwood. If you find one with a boxed-in base or a low hanging "apron" of wood, lift the seat to discover the commode compartment below.

Pieces from a mid-19th century bone chess set of 'Barleycorn' type.

Oil lamps

For years collectors converted their oil finds to take electricity. Now the emphasis is on owning lamps in the original condition. The development of oil lamps is closely connected with the type of fuel used. Colza (vegetable oil) lamps appeared after 1873 and paraffin was first refined in 1847. The cheaper 19th century oil lamps had milky white (opal) oil reservoirs or founts, often painted over with floral designs. The heavy cast iron base or foot was frequently ornamented and engraved. A better model might feature a gleaming brass pillar support standing on a black ceramic base. The oil fount might be green, blue, amber or ruby colored glass in these more expensive versions. The dearest lamps stood on pillars like those in a Greek temple and founts of cut glass were common. There were also hand lamps for use in the bedroom, piano lamps which sat in the candle sconce that swung out to throw light on the player's score, harp lamps that hung from the ceiling suspended in elegant lyre-shaped metal frames, and standard lamps, often with telescopic adjustments for use as a reading or room light.

10

Looking At And Looking After Your Collection

Display cases

Genuine antique cases and cabinets are notoriously hard to come by. Everyone wants them: the collector, because he knows that a well thought out arrangement on silk or baize in a display cabinet can greatly enhance his collection; and the dealer needs them too, because a fine display in his shop window can help him sell more. A purpose-built period display cabinet is a great joy to own. Basically they divide into two types, for books and for china or small collectables. Cabinets with glazed side panels are more likely to be for objects, not books: for there is no necessity to read the outside cover of the first and last volumes in a row of library bound books, as all the information, such as title and author, is contained in gilt lettering on the spines which can be easily viewed from the front. A further clue can be found in the back panelling of display cabinets. With a china display, the back would itself be on show and is likely to be of a finer finish than if it were concealed by a phalanx of books. Elaborate glazing bars may also indicate the china cabinet, as books were more likely to have simple up and down rectangular styles of barring, to make it easier to decipher the titles behind glass. Collectors who cannot lay their hands on suitable display cabinets are often forced to improvize, and often do so successfully and

A fine 19th century heavily carved oak display cabinet.

cheaply. One of the most satisfactory solutions is to remove the wood panelling in the doors of ancient or damaged and second-rate cabinets and replace them with glass. Clocks and other vertical collectables can be conveniently and attractively capped with the glass domes that once protected a stuffed animal or dried flower display. The Edwardian glass-topped display table is useful for small items like jewelry, potlids, or lace. A Victorian music cabinet, perhaps in

154

walnut and with a brass gallery, could be raised high to make a novel display cabinet.

If you find the shelving too deep in your impromptu cabinet you could cover a number of cardboard or wooden boxes in attractive cloth, such as velvet or satin, and arrange them on the shelves as rests for your objects, building up and forward to diminish the depth. Buff-colored linen suits china, while green is curiously apt for "blue and white" pottery, and glass looks exceptionally well on lace. It helps create imaginary lines of sight by arranging, for example, a group of jugs, or steins, smallest in the front and largest at the back: the diminishing size exaggerates perspective and gives the illusion of space.

Polish your pieces well first and it is a good idea if you wear chamois gloves when handling glassware to keep it absolutely free of fingerprints.

A concoction of detergent liquid in an egg cup full of ammonia lifts dirt out of scratches in glazed items which can then be polished with a smear of proprietary furniture polish. Beware of lighting inside cabinets. A light left on too long could crack a delicate piece of porcelain, a highly stressed material. (This can be seen when a piece of porcelain is broken and it is almost impossible to marry the parts afterwards.) The best lighting idea is to have the lamps switch on automatically as you enter the room and switch off as you leave. Glass shelving is a good idea, as it helps keep your wattage to a minimum by letting light penetrate to the depths of your cabinet.

You may decide to forgo the pleasures of a perpetual and easily visible display in favor of greater safety from fire and prying fingers. One collector with a hoard of tsuba abandoned all attempts at an open display. His collection rests on black felt in the trays of what is really a tall metal cabinet designed for office stationery. It provides quick access for private study, is also fairly fireproof and, most important of all, is lockable—a point which might deter the less determined thief.

Displaying bottles

Single bottles look good in isolation on a shelf preferably high up, facing a window. Glass needs light and can make a stunning display on a window ledge, or as ornaments on a shelving room divider. The subtle shades of stoneware ginger beer bottles are best appreciated

COLLECTING FOR FUN & PROFIT
COLLECTING FOR FUN & PROFIT

outside a glazed cabinet and look especially attractive in an open shelf pine corner cupboard.

Glass

Bottle collectors who dig up their bottles know all about sick glass. It is a reaction caused by chemicals in the soil which can permanently damage the glass giving it a frosted opaque look (though where the frosting has progressed sufficiently to make the glass irridescent this is considered highly desirable). Glass that has not been mistreated can also suffer merely because the original proportion of ingredients in the melt was incorrect. Professional polishing can remove marks from the outside of glass, but the inside of a bottle is often impossible to reach. You can gloss over the problem. Take a twig and attach a piece of cotton wool or cloth to one end; soak in a high grade clear mineral oil and rub over the marks until they disappear (at least to look at). The bottle then needs to be tightly corked to prevent evaporation of the oil. But the trick can hold good for years.

Decanters and flasks are a different kettle of fish. People want to use them, not just look at them. Sediment, a common problem, should respond to soap and water soakings; if not try a mild solution of either vinegar and water or washing soda in water. Alkali (soda) should be used to combat acid stains, and vice versa. Another course of action, for sediment that refuses to shift, is to fill quarter-way with water and a small quantity of steel shot, bird tray litter, or sand. Lead is not recommended as it is not sharp enough and may coat the vessel with lead and ruin it. A further suggestion that I have yet to try is to use denture cleaner; but do a test first.

Marble

Some advise against using even mild soap on marble because it can destroy that lovely translucent patina that develops with antique marble. But all the authorities agree that dust, soot and iron particles are the chief enemies of marble and that regular light brushing with a soft bristle or feather duster is a good idea. Marble is porous, and especially vulnerable to penetrating iron oxide—rust. Pale marble may even pick up the traces from a rusty bucket used to carry the washing solution and the pigment from a colored cleaning cloth, so use white cotton or cottonwool. Standing a glass of wine, bottle of vinegar or lemon juice will have a damaging effect on marble which is susceptible to acids. Smears and dribbles of dirty solution are to be avoided, so start from the bottom and work your way upwards, drying with a soft, clean white cloth as you go. A mild solution of hydrogen peroxide, perhaps with a drop or two of ammonia added, will remove ink. Serious stains may need repolishing or other professional attention.

Ceramics

The more delicate and valuable the object the more cautiously you will treat it. Warm water (very hot can encourage crazing) and soap or washing-up liquid is almost universally suitable. With less important porcelain or earthenware you may risk bleach which can appear to remove cracks just because it discolors the dirt in the crack that makes it show. But steeping a cracked item in a bleach solution can result in serious expansion of the flaw. A more gentle bleaching action is obtainable from hydrogen peroxide solution (one part 100 volumes hydrogen peroxide to three parts water, plus a drop of ammonia). Prior soaking in distilled water for a few hours will help prevent the stain from going deeper in. Food stains may respond to bleaching or to the use of a foaming denture cleaner: test a small unobtrusive part first. Still on the tooth idea, you can make good use of a clean old toothbrush to scrub at broken edges. Always rinse in clean water and dry with a silk cloth, which is lint free. Fruit and ink stains can be tackled with damp household salt on a hard paste porcelain. Rust remover can be used and should be cleaned off completely with acetone once the rust stain has gone.

Silver

The manufactured dips are popular for small items like jewelry but large items will need plate powder of the highest quality: soft enough not to scratch, yet stout enough to tackle discoloration and tarnish. Remember that silver is a soft metal, so especial care should be taken with raised (embossed) surfaces. Even if an item is too large for dipping, but has indentations that make it impossible to remove the black sulphide using powder, place it in a plastic bowl, dab it all over with cotton wool soaked in the dip—but make sure you wear plastic gloves. Then remove the white coating with silver polish and a soft cloth. Stubborn patches can be defeated with a mixture of jeweller's rouge and water or chalk and water; work into engraving or repoussé work with a stiff hair brush (not metal).

Bronze

It is a mistake to clean bronze antiques to the gleaming "newness" of copper or brass. The patination of ages should be preserved, although dirt must be removed with soapy water and a soft brush. Rinse and then dry in a current of warm, dry air then treat with a preparation of melted beeswax. Brush off excess wax and buff with a soft cloth.

Pewter

The quality of pewter may dictate how much harsh treatment you can –or should–give it. Cheap grade pewter will have a high lead content. Check this by rubbing a sharp edge of the item against a white card; pure tin (the finest pewter is an alloy of about 112 parts tin to 25 parts copper or, in "tin and temper" one per cent antimony, without the copper) will leave almost no trace. High lead pewter will write almost as clearly as a pencil. In old times pewter was kept in a gleaming state by scrubbing with oil and rotten-stone or sand and rushes. Today it can be polished with silversand or whiting; but take it easy, as you may remove the touch marks, vital clues to dating authenticity.

Copper

Like brass, but unlike silver, copper responds best to treatment with a slightly abrasive polish. Inconsequential scratches can be dealt with using jeweller's rouge. Something grossly marred by verdigris requires a heavier hand. Strong bleach in boiling water often works, if the item can be submerged. A metal scouring pad or a powder cleaner will remove the more stubborn patches. One folk recipe suggests sea salt partially dissolved in boiling vinegar, the crystals act as an abrasive. Do not let the liquid dribble over the copper.

Brass

At its worst brass becomes covered in a greenish overcoat of grime and chemical decomposition. Immerse in a strong solution of washing up liquid, warm water and ammonia, rubbing from time to time with a fine brass wire brush. The brass will then look brassy but dull, and can be polished using a standard cleaner.

Iron

Cast iron, notoriously brittle, requires careful handling; it also tends to be attacked by rust more severely than does wrought iron. Fine wire wool and oil copes with all but the deepest rust. An item that is truly beyond hope of being cleaned by hand or electric drill, with metal brush attachment, may have to be sand-blasted, after which it ceases to look antique but may well become an attractive decorator item.

Furniture

Woodworm used to be cleared from furniture by placing it in a fumigating chamber which was then sealed and filled with cyanide and carbon di-sulphide gas. Not only does this method carry obvious health hazards, but the gas did not always penetrate sufficiently to kill the creature deep inside the wood. Female woodworm (or furniture beetle) lays its eggs in any cranny - knot, crack, nail or keyhole - and the grub then tunnels for two years into the wood where it turns into a chrysalis and then into an adult. The neat circular holes are left by the emerging adult. Woodworm prefers sapwood and will tackle hard varieties like oak or mahogany as well as soft pine. Pine is often devastated by it, but the worm sometimes appears to give up on mahogany and tough oak as a bad job. Almost any old furniture will have worm holes; it is a normal sign of age and is nothing to get upset about. But live worm must be gotten rid of right away, before it not only spreads within the piece but, worse still, infects other furniture. Sharp edges to the flight holes may indicate that the worm is still active. Tap the furniture to see if a fine sawdust escapes – a sure-fire sign that worm still lives. There is a choice of insecticides that can be squirted into the flight holes, joints and cracks. And it helps if you can turn the piece so that gravity works for you as well. Brush over the undersides as an added precaution.

The ideal insecticide will be non-staining: this you can check on an unexposed piece. Odorless products appear to be a luxury. I treated a table successfully ten years ago but it still stinks. After treatment the holes can be stopped with beeswax and turpentine or, more conveniently, with colored shoe polish. Shoe polish is such a valued standby of the odd-jobbing dealer and collector that one French manufacturer of shoe polish brought out a range of polish specifically for woodworkers.

Paper collectables

Ephemera such as cigarette cards, playing cards, bookmarks, should never be stuck into a scrapbook or they will be ruined. Even the tiny translucent mounts used for postage stamps are unsuitable. One of the neatest methods of holding paper or card exhibits in place is to lightly pencil the corners, to indicate the dimensions, then cut a diagonal snick in the paper of the album leaf and insert the ephemera rather like photographs are held in purpose-made photographic albums. You can also buy stick-on corners or make them yourself by cutting obliquely across the corners of old envelopes. Plastic sleeved display sheets are fine for photographic transparencies, but may be hazardous to early printing: the plastic can seal in moisture or mold. Paper-backed plastic can be found to avoid this problem. Plastic with an acid content can also be damaging, according to a dealer in stocks and bonds.

Pine

Pine collectors often like to buy their pieces in a rough state because the stripping and repair work is often within the grasp of even the most unhandy handyman. Small or delicate pieces can be stripped using a proprietary stripper. But these, as well as the professional method of dunking the pine in a vat of a caustic soda solution, should be handled with respect and care. Professional tips for successful pine stripping include having as deep a bath as possible (one dealer has his five foot deep, seven foot across and 10 foot long); it is important, too, not to overheat the liquid or immerse the pine over-long. Drawers should be removed and stripped separately, and so should other pieces which might prevent the furniture being stripped all over, like catches and doors. Do not leave pine furniture soaking too long: a half-hour can often be sufficient; some professionals prefer to "dunk" three or four times with an interval in between. Too long can lead to crystals forming on the backs of pieces and inside drawers when the furniture begins to dry out. After immersion thorough washing is a must: a good hosing down with water is essential.

Full preparation of pine is a time-consuming and energetic business. You will need to rub down with wax a couple of times a week for six or seven weeks and work over the piece with wire wool. Burnishing and exposure to air bring up the grain and the knots and help improve the patina. You can buy ready-made polishes but one of the best is a mixture, equal parts by weight, of turpentine and beeswax. White spirit can be used but it may crystalize the polish. Turpentine is a natural oil, cheap too, and imparts a handsome sheen to pine.

11
Shopping For Antiques

Are you bold enough to make a success of antiques? Whether as a collector, a dealer or a part-time trader you will have to buy from people and also sell. Unless you can barter intelligently and effectively you may never achieve your collecting ambition or earn as much money as is your due.

There is no need to be brash or aggressive: market trading in antiques is not like selling nylons or china seconds. You won't need to attract the attention of your customers with a histrionic display: if your stock is right shoppers will find you. And if your prices are right they will buy. But be warned: antiques is no place for the shy person—not unless you can turn that trepidation into a money-making trick.

One dealer who finds it upsetting to be constantly badgered by professional and private customers trying to knock points off the marked price pretends the shop isn't hers. She says it is her friend's; the most her friend the dealer "allows" her to forego on the marked price is 10 per cent. And she never knows when her friend, the owner, will be back . . .

Every selling and buying ploy will be tempered by its success or otherwise in the field. That woman maintains her front because she has enough trade with customers who will accept her modest discount. She can afford to kiss goodbye to the greater turnover she would no doubt have if she were less timorous and could adopt a more flexible trading policy. As I write is is easier for many dealers to sell than it is for them to replace stock. There is a finite number of desirable items available, ranging from the indisputably antique to knick-knacks that would bring a glint to the eye of the collector of Rock 'n' Roll memorabilia. But they appear to have become spread rather thinly.

There has never been a comparable market in antiques; no-one can confidently predict the outcome. Nevertheless, there are certain immutable "laws" of the market place that should hearten the antiques fraternity.

Whether we like it, or acknowledge it, or not, we all lower our sights in accordance with our expectations. Ideally we should all be million-aires and married to filmstars, with a six-figure annual clothing budget! But we are not. Yet the world seems to manage just the same — indeed, there is a population explosion.

Oak chairs from the reign of King Charles 11 (just picture those barley sugar twist legs and you'll known what I mean), Deco bronzes with luscious ladies baring svelte ivory limbs, and fine Old Sheffield Plate have all disappeared beyond the reach of the average dealer. They haven't gone for good. They have gone up-market. They may end up in a museum, languish for a while in a swank gallery, thanks to an unspeakable price tag, or find grace in a collector's cabinet. But they will be back some day. Collectors die; they change their minds; they complete their self-imposed collecting assignments. Nothing is surer.

With prices rising, a fresh search for "new" collectables is inevitable, as is a cheese-paring scrutiny of the old ones to see how they can be further subdivided to intrigue collectors. One of the more bizarre recent vogues must be that of collecting old record labels. At last! No need to worry about the playability of a disc or the lack of a suitable talking machine.

The trick is to be clued-up sufficiently to be able to buy advantageously the instant a golden opportunity presents itself. A dealer friend complained recently about a customer who had wanted to buy the most insignificant item on her stand, a brass boat with a $1 price tag. The customer wanted to know if she could have it for 75 cents because, she said, she was trying to buy stuff to resell for a charity, which she named. Needless to say, my friend did not believe her story. "But what did you do?" I asked. "I sold it to her for 75 cents," the dealer said, glumly, and continued to curse the customer who was probably, but not necessarily, lying, and who had managed to screw an unpalatable 25 per cent discount out of my friend.

Yet both had acted properly: a deal had been struck. But let me repeat, if you need to lie to satisfy your conscience; or have trade cards printed for a ficitious establishment to justify your ineffective verbal demands for a professional discount; if you find trading sets hairs on end–then maybe you would be better off in some less forceful activity than dealing or even the higher reaches of collecting, where constant trading up is a necessity.

If you are still with me, here are some tricks to help you stay the course.

The money mentality

Almost all casual transactions with antiques are done for cash. A long standing customer with a regular turnover of business with a particular dealer, or a buyer at auction will settle with a scrawled signature, but normally it's banknotes. And many establishments now accept credit cards. By the way, once you know that plastic money organizations take a cut of perhaps 5 per cent, for their service, you can turn this to good advantage with a tricky dealer who carries a window sticker to indicate that he accepts a range of plastic. If he refuses to come down to a price that you consider fair and reasonable you can "threaten" to pay with your credit card on which he will lose a further 5 per cent. It must make sense, you insist, for him to let you chop off that extra 5 per cent and pay cash.

There are risks, however. You may irritate him so much he refuses to do business with you thereafter. And at any time he can refuse to sell. For having an item displayed and even price-tagged is not part of a contract to sell; there is no obligation. Juggle with price tags by all means; but juggle gently.

How to work with cash

Cash dealing is quite an art. The first step is to arm yourself with a full variety of denominations of notes and big coins. These you plant about your person. One pocket might have dollar bills, pound notes or French francs, another $20 bills or £10 notes, and so on. But each pocket has a combination of rolled-up bundles, which you can make a show of producing, and folded singles of the same denomination: it would be fatal to be bargaining hard over a single dollar and then produce a great wad of notes. Similarly, you must remember where everything is so you do not produce the wrong amount of money at a critical moment.

First you need to break the code the dealer sometimes uses to price his goods. (In passing, from a dealer's point of view it must be bad news not to price goods. He should remind himself how he reacts, for example, to an exclusive-looking couture shop where the beautiful displays are not priced; the goods are probably dammed expensive, he assumes! Exactly, dummy!! So unless there is some mileage in promoting that belief — and I cannot think what that could be—it must be an advantage to use even a coded price tag.)

Some dealers appreciate this and will use a code so obvious it can be broken by all but the moribund: A=1, B=2, C=3, and so on. Or he might start further along the alphabet to confuse things a bit.

One dealer uses a five-figure code in which the first and last numerals are discarded and 11 subtracted from the total to arrive at the price. For lower value articles a four-figure code is used. Price codes prevent comparison shopping by both professional and amateur; they also stymie members of the public anxious to put a price tag on their own goods. But with more and more dealers forced to stay out on the road to replenish hard-to-come-by stock, codes may just be a means to help hired staff trade without trauma.

What is the point of using a code? Well, one of the problems dealers with a big stock have is knowing what price everything is; they simply forget. And nothing is more irritating to a customer than the dealer who say's he's forgotten how much something was and he'll have to consult his notebook. Disbelief and suspicion descend. So the numbers/letters may refer not to the asking price but to the buying price. In other words, what appeared to be a straightforward buying code now becomes a much more subtle tool of the trade.

What a dealer paid for an item is immutable, logged in history; what he plans to ask for it is a variable. This is a simple fact of the market place (stores and emporia included). If you don't believe it try asking a dealer in a busy Sunday market how much something is early in the morning and later in the day. The price often goes down as the dealer lowers his sights in favor of not having to cart that particular object away and bring it back the following week. Prices go up and down in accordance with many additional factors—such as your apparent financial status (no amount of tatty denims will disguise the Cartier Tank watch on your wrist); your standing as "trade" or private customer; and how much your total bill is likely to be if you buy a group of things (more of this later).

Sometimes the price code will spell out what you are entitled to as trade. Theoretically that should save time wasting and nerve jangling haggling. But it may not if you think you can improve on what is offered. One lady dealer whom I worked hard on to clinch a deal at a more favorable price kept complaining, as I tightened the screw, "I'm going to be sick, I feel sick." But she wasn't. She just stuck in the huffy way that indicates that you really have reached rock bottom. Then we dealt. They say that Arab traders in the souk get genuinely disappointed if you don't bargain with them. Dealers are often, but not always, cast in the same mold.

Given that you want to pay as little as possible for your purchases, what is the best way to go about it? It is a fact that there is more business done between dealers than between dealer and private customer; goods go the rounds from dealer to dealer, perhaps dropping off at the auction room, spiraling up through the classier showrooms (if it is a top-notch piece of furniture, for example), and then on to the home of a stockbroker, or the villa of a fancy actress in Florence. The dealer will try to help the fellow dealer by leaving him "another turn" in the price: selling at a price which can be reasonably easily improved upon in the next sale. A dealer who is not getting a price he can work with will complain that the "price isn't right" or "There's nothing in it for me", indicating that he won't be able to turn it over himself for a profit, quick or otherwise.

So it was that from the Sixties onwards any Tom, Dick or Harriet would shuffle around antique shops or look askance at goods on the trader's stand and ask, "What's the trade price on that?" Or: "What's your best price on...?" The former demands that the customer be deemed to qualify as trade; the latter implies that the price, far from being the "best price", may indeed be the worst. Having to choose between an act of faith and an insult, not surprisingly the dealer baulks at the prospect, and the buyer is unlikely to get a favorable response. Buying at a trade discount price may carry an unwanted penalty; it could invoke the mercantile principle of *caveat emptor:* let the buyer beware. Having made your purchase you must abide by your judgment.

Because there are so many coming into the trade these days, part-timers and market traders who hold down respectable jobs during the week, the distinction between a private and a trade buyer has became blurred. Current thinking is that the come-on that best bridges the gap is: "What's the best you can do on...?" The buyer understands that there may be some difficulty involved, given the state of the art, the recent hike in the mortgage rate, and so on, and appreciates the effort. The "you" also somehow personalizes the deal, the goods fall in-to second place; this is a communion between people, the dealer is not a crane-like robot in an amusement arcade picking things up and depositing them in the right slot. He, or she, is a human being. And being human he, or she, is open to persuasion - and temptation.

"A fire-mark sold at Christie's for £260 ($600)."

Suppose you have established your credentials as serious buyer. Your eyes light up at the prospect of three items on a Paris dealer's stand. You want all of them. But how do you work out the best deal? Imagine a tea pot for 100 Francs, a crested china bottle for 50 Francs and a brass tray at 150 Francs. First estimate the sort of discount you might expect. On the teapot it could be 10 Francs, on the bottle, 5 Francs and on the brass tray 15 to 20 Francs. All of which is speculative, depending on trade that day generally, what the dealer had for breakfast, and so on. You might get nothing, but you could reasonably expect to get those amounts knocked off without busting a gut.

So how do you improve in the deal? You must start with an item on which the dealer has something worthwhile going for him, like the tea-pot. Ask him what is the best he can do on it. Suppose he sticks at 90 Francs. Suggest you might be interested in the bottle, too, if the price is right. He says you can have it for 45 Francs. So offer him 130 Francs for the two items and pass over two 50s, holding back the rest. Now indicate that you might be interested in the brass tray as well. What can he do on that? He may say you can have it for 140 or 130. Pull out another three 50s and offer him 250 in all.

To a man who had originally expected to receive just a couple more tens and who is now on the receiving end of five 50s, the prospect could prove irresistible. You will have gotten the tray for 120, 10 Francs better than his best price, and the bottle for the extra 5 off that he had not even agreed to.

With practise you may be able to work out all sorts of complex accumulating deals—and then slice another bit off the total.

Buying at auction

A catalog is usually issued a few weeks before an auction sale. How well you read and understand it may determine your success or otherwise in the saleroom and, long-term, your collecting and dealing career. First flick through the catalog, glancing over each page. Unconsciously you will be mentally logging items that interest. Then go back to the beginning and READ THE SMALL PRINT, especially the sections called "Conditions of sale" or "Standard notices". There may be a glossary to help you understand how the lots have been categorized, or a list of the books used as reference; a key to descriptive words, such as "proof" or "extremely fine", in a coin sale; and other little gems such as "All lots are sold as shown, with all faults, imperfections and errors of description." There is often more protection for the private person purchasing from a dealer than there is in the saleroom. Damaged goods can be referred to as "AF"- bought "as found". "Not subject to return" is another phrase to watch.

The way an item is cataloged is of acute importance, especially with pictures. A painting ascribed to "Sir Peter Paul Rubens" is, as far as the saleroom is concerned, the real thing. A picture labeled "Rubens" is, probably, a copy. "In the style of Rubens" could be auction house jargon for a fake.

The saleroom buff also studies any "literature" referred to. This can mean a reference to a book or an article which mentions the picture or item in question, a certificate testifying to the authenticity of the lot, usually written by an art scholar, or a private letter naming the goods. An abundance of literature is often, but not necessarily, good news. When you check out the references, you may discover the item has been the subject of controversy. In the Depression even eminent art historians peddled favorable written opinions (certificates) for cash. A letter, preferably from an authority, is often more highly regarded, since it was probably unsolicited.

Even the typography of the catalog description is revealing. Any lot meriting a page to itself and with a bold heading is considered an important item by the auctioneers. Block capital letters at the start of a description tell a similar story. Star lots are often illustrated, though lesser lots can be, too, just to show the scope of a sale–and remember that the seller usually pays for the photograph and may be delighted to do so if he feels it will enhance his cash prospects.

A lot may be headed: "THE PROPERTY OF ...", followed by the name of an officer in the armed forces, a famous personality, and so on. More intriguing is the strapline, "THE PROPERTY OF A GENTLEMAN" or "THE PROPERTY OF A LADY OF TITLE". In the past "BY ORDER OF A NOBLEMAN" or "REMOVED FROM A MANSION IN THE COUNTRY" were popular, for snobbery sells. More to the point, however, is the likelihood that these goods are fresh on the market, not trade goods which may have been in and out of the saleroom over the years. There may also be a list of previous owners. The "provenance" or pedigree can help the price along. Famous collectors of the past marked their possessions and,given the collector's standing, this can be the equivalent of an authentication.

A saleroom bargain is no more than an unestablished work. Before the true quality can be revealed–and value realized–time-consuming research may be required. So that when a noted dealer or connoisseur collector is bidding for an apparently minor lot this is sometimes as good as an authentication, and less *au fait* bidders will join the fray.

Understated catalog decriptions are used by the auctioneers to tempt buyers. Some of the usually easily accessible literature is omitted,. in the hope that the curious will "discover" something and be encouraged to pay over the top in the heat of the moment.

Salerooms often issue a printed list of estimates, a range of prices which they expect the lots to attain. If there is no written estimate, ask for a verbal one. The price guides are a fair indication of hammer prices, but they should be used with caution. The lapse between printing and writing dates may be as much as a year, time enough for saleroom prices to become wildly out of date. Average prices are also hard to come by. A hammer price may have been freakishly depressed because of the activities of the ring (of which more later) or because a wealthy collector was determined to bag the lot—at any price.

Some old auction hands mark a price that they are prepared to go to on everything in a catalog. The best lots are often left to the end, for obvious reasons, and you can pick up resaleable items cheaply when dealers begin to lose interest or run out of money. Often the lot which immediately precedes and the lot which follows an important item will get less attention than it merits because of the build-up and subsequent furore. The sharp operator takes advantage of such distractions or any momentary lapse of concentration.

The importance of viewing

Never buy anything you haven't viewed. At the view, held usually for a couple of days before the sale or just on the morning of the auction, thoroughly inspect the lots that interest you, and preferably everything else as well. If something is locked away in a case, ask the attendant to fetch it out. Always handle porcelain: it is often easier to spot a repair with a fingertip or a fingernail than with the eye. Tip chairs over to see the construction. An unscrupulous carpenter can turn one period chair into two by splicing on artifically aged wood. Try to see every lot: the one you miss could be the bargain. Country sales are notorious for lots that need to be ferreted out, someone may have hidden something away for his own purposes. Always ask for what you want to see and keep asking until you get it.

If a lot contains several items, check that everything described is present. Things disappear at views; reassure yourself that everything is present and correct before bidding. Even after a successful bid the danger is not over. It is often a good idea to tip an attendant to keep an eye on things on your behalf. It is easy for a villain to transfer prime items from your box of mixed junk to his.

Reserves

The auctioneer is professionally bound not to reveal the reserve - the price below which the vendor will not sell. But you may be able to squeeze the information out of a porter, though it is against the rules. The estimate is yours for the asking. The top estimate is often, but not always, about a third more than the reserve.Close to the sale you may be told an estimate and also informed that you will be unlikely to get it for that price. This could indicate strong interest in the lot, or it could mean that there is already a "bid on the book" (a bid left with the clerk by an interested party who cannot be present) which tops the estimate.

Where a client insists on too high a reserve, the estimate may be pitched on the low side, so as not to put off potential buyers.

It is easy to get carried away by the drama and excitement of the saleroom, to bid too much—a reason why it is important to mark the catalog with the maximum you are prepared to pay. This you stick to except for one bid: it would be a pity to miss out on a good deal just because the bidding was down to the other guy at your penciled-in limit. As a general rule, it is better to regret having bought than to regret not having bought. And remember, your accumulated catalogs, marked with prices achieved, the estimates and your own purchases, are your form books for future fortune; keep them safe.

The best way to bid

Bidding successfully at auction is not only within reach of wealthy dealers and collectors. At auctions held by even the most prestigious houses, on average over half of the lots go for a few hundred or less. And in spite of those spoofs in which an old master is knocked down to the man with an itchy nose, the normal practise is to make absolutely clear to the auctioneer that you are bidding. Raising a hand, a gesture with a rolled-up catalog, or a nod are all normal and acceptable signals. The problems start when you want to conceal your interest in a lot. You may fear that a rival dealer will "run you up"

–force the bidding higher to make you pay more. He may want to cut down your spending power to keep you out of the running for a later lot that you both fancy. And malice sometimes plays a part. At big city sales it may be possible to arrange a bidding code with the auctioneer. A simple one might be that the auctioneer's clerk is to bid on your behalf as long as you have your spectacles on, but that he is to stop the instant you remove them. Be careful not to let them slip!

Remember an auctioneer will aim to clear anything up to 90 or 120 lots an hour; asking him to remember an obscure charade is not a good idea. The auctioneer may forget the plot and you could come embarrassingly, if not financially, unstuck. Although you are legally liable to pay for a lot that is knocked down to you, you will rarely be asked to stump up for a genuine error. Conversely, if the hammer comes down and you are still in the running, then say out loud, "I am still bidding". Better than a bidding code may be to pass the bid to a colleague who will carry on bidding on your behalf.

Be sure you know how the bidding is likely to advance. Normally the steps will be in units of 2 or 3 for inexpensive items, to 5 a bid; in the low hundreds each bid could be a tenner; in the low thousands 100, and on up to units of a thousand per consective bid or more. But the auctioneer has a free hand to call the shots, to accept a lesser "pushing" bid, if it suits the mood of the moment. You can also leave a bid with a porter (who will need to be tipped and suitably rewarded if he succeeds on your behalf). The advantage here is that his experience will tell him the best point at which he can insert your bid. Or you could get a dealer to bid on your behalf. The risk of leaving a bid on the book is that the auctioneer could start bidding dangerously close to your bid, even though he ought to let you have the lot for as little as possible, bearing in mind the level of interest in the saleroom. Picking bids off the wall is another unfortunate trick of the trade. Most auction houses turn a blind eye to fictional bids being snatched from thin air to boost the price. If the rhythm of bidding changes, this could mean that the walls have started bidding!

Saleroom types: the ring

When several dealers are in competition for the same lot a ring may be formed. Rather than bid against each other they combine to buy cheap and resolve the conflict independently. The group elects a spokesman or chairman, generally the most financially important among them, to be the front man; he bids. Having secured the lot the ring gathers, perhaps at a local bar or car park, for the "knock-out".

Here the chairman auctions the goods again, starting at the price reached in the saleroom.

If the goods were originally knocked down for $200 and at the ring's auction they make $600, then the new buyer pays out $400. This is divided equally among the members other than himself. The new owner also reimburses the chairman his $200 (which has been paid to the auctioneer's clerk and is all the vendor will receive for his goods).

Suppose there are five in the ring: four share $400—a pleasant way to pick up $100. For that reason the lowest form of life in the antiques trade haunt auction rooms just on the off-chance of being included in a ring. They often are, simply for their nuisance value—the danger of their running up prices out of spite, for instance.

With top quality goods, like important paintings, a further round of bidding may follow. This usually consists of bona fide interested parties only. The ring is a conspiracy to defraud the vendor and is illegal, but little can be done to prevent rings forming. The best way for the vendor to confound the ring is to see that his lot carries a sensible reserve. An amateur who tries to beat the ring in the saleroom can sometimes find himself run up, hassled, or his goods mysteriously damaged—all out of spite.

The follower

The follower, usually a specialist collector, waits for a dealer to place his final bid and then tops it. The follower knows that if he wants to buy that item from the dealer's shop he will have to pay perhaps twice the price the dealer paid at auction to accommodate the latter's profit margin. A frustrated dealer can retaliate by forcing up the price - and then dropping out.

Bargains from bad weather

Bad weather keeps competition down and may keep the trade away altogether at remote salerooms. Advantageous buying is often possible before a national holiday, at the end or beginning of the season, and in August when dealers are on holiday.

Selling at auction

Most auctioneers will give a free, verbal, over-the-counter valuation without obligation. In special cases, a valuer will travel short distances, free, if you appear to be a serious vendor. Out-of-town visits are usually charged. The valuer may say he would like to see a photograph before he can comment. They usually prefer black and white prints as the colors of a cheap print can be deceiving, though transparencies may suit.

How quickly a lot can be included in a sale is of acute importance. Furniture is easily placed in a general sale, a frequent event. Specialist items, such as fans or dolls, may be kept back for a collectors' sale, to allow time for the auction house to muster a worthwhile selection and contact collectors worldwide. But it may mean months of waiting for the goods to come under the hammer.

Telephone the saleroom to discover minimum charges per lot, how much the vendor pays if a lot fails to reach its reserve, fee for cataloging, illustration, insurance, size of commission, and so on.

The auctioneer having accepted your goods for sale will want to quickly agree a reserve. Do not be pressed; it may be possible to wait to see what interest there is in your goods and set a more realistic reserve than if you made a quick judgment.

The shrewd antique buyer thinks laterally

In a market you are in competition with everyone for what the stall holder has on show. There may be something more interesting that he has not yet put out. Perhaps he is waiting for other items to go to clear a space. Meanwhile he keeps it under the stall, perhaps wrapped in newspaper. Some of the best finds are made in this way.

Another trick. Almost all dealers use some kind of showcase, whatnot or stand to rest their goods on. Everyone looks at the goods, not the surround. It's a bit like the story about the mantlepiece and stoking the fire: there may be something very interesting on the mantlepiece. A dealer may need to be encouraged with an over-the-odds offer before he will relinquish part of his display equipment, however.

Money found

Walking along the street one day I noticed a nicely turned leg protruding from a truck full of builder's waste. I didn't run for the police; it wasn't a human limb but a polished mahogany leg with a battered old castor attached to one end and what appeared to be a folding table top on the other. The builders were excavating an old house to turn it into a cheap hotel. "Is the boss around?" I asked the workman in the hall. The boss never appeared but the messenger ferried back my query about the table. "Have it", came the reply. Have it! The man was mad. For when I pulled the table out it was clearly all there; a bit loose around the hinges, perhaps, and with traces of hot pans having been stood on a plastic tablecloth on the table top, having been used to mix paint on and such like, but otherwise undamaged. The craftsmen who worked on the table said there was $100 worth of mahogany in it. New castors were easy to buy—with more time I might have poked around the rummage box of a junk dealer and come up with suitable period ones. My mid 19th century Sutherland table, for that is what it was, beautifully refurbished, would now sell for $450. "Ask. And ye shall receive," is a wise old antique-finder's motto.

Professional tips for amateur sellers

Some of the most successful newspaper small ads for antiques carry pictures, often no more than a thumbnail sketch of a grandfather clock or desk. The tag line reads: "Do you have a clock like this?". How do I know they are successful ads? They keep on appearing - and with the price of advertising space that must mean that they are working.

The main hook, however, is your headline. Always give a card a bold heading—and underline it, preferably in a contrasting color. "OLD CLOCK, PENDULUM MISSING", "THIRTIES TEA SET". You don't need to become an advertising copywriter to get the message across effectively. Short, sharp, sentences and phrases are needed, just like a telegram: "PINE DRESSER. SOUND BUT PAINTED, PERFECT FOR STRIPPING. ORIGINAL HANDLES."

Snapshots are good to use. But simple black sketches are just as good or better. If you can't draw, follow the lines on a similar item in one of the price guides. When you put in the price, always add the "o.n.o." (or near offer). Everyone likes to negotiate, and nowhere more than in the antiques game.

The card that you make up, your master copy, should be clear and all black type. This you take to the photocopier. Later you can add color with a fibre tip pen.

The best way to run a window card campaign is to saturate an area. Use all the stationer's shops, post offices, etc., in your area. Put the cards in on the same day, preferably in the middle of the week, as the shopkeeper will often refuse to put them up on a busy Friday—and Saturday is your best day, the day shopping areas carry most pedestrian traffic.

Window cards can work wonders—for dealers, too. I've known the bizarre situation where a dealer, pretending to be a private seller advertises in a shop window—and ends up selling to another dealer pretending to be a private buyer!

Secret antiques, the cheapest antiques of all . . .

When you come across old books, magazines, postcard albums, always study them carefully. Tucked inside, there may be a relic worth the asking price many times over. I once invested a few coins in a 1919 book I didn't even want because folded up inside was a poster advertising an end-of-war victory celebration. To a specialist, that poster is worth money. A lot of people kept postage stamps tucked in books; you may find a valuable early issue in mint condition. The backs of old desks and bureaux are other good places to look for lost stamps.

Old letters sometimes come to light. The stamp on the envelope may be worthless, but the postmark could earn cash. These "accidental" antiques are a free bonus. Everyone else is usually too intent on looking at the outside of things to spot the snip inside.

Take an old upholstered 'Grandfather chair' in a second-hand shop. Our great grandparents were just as likely to lose things down the backs of chairs as we are. Hidden in the springs and stuffing you may find valuable old coins, a penknife, keys, or a silver cufflink.

Antique dealer Jean Anderson tells of a man who picked up an old oak chest for a small sum at auction: "The lid was locked and no one could budge it, so they sold it as it was. Later, the owner forced the lock and discovered, well wrapped up inside, thousands worth of Georgian silver."

True stories of fabulous finds abound, and add spice to the business of selling and collecting antiques. It would be a foolish person, however, who, hoping to get rich quick, "prospected" for hidden treasure. But it would be equally daft not to look in those places where people are known to have hidden valuable objects. Particularly intriguing are the secret places in bureaux, desks and writing slopes where cash and valuables were hidden in the absence of safes and banks. Simple measurements of cavities may reveal a hidden compartment. Some of these hidey holes were ingeniously fastened with secret spring catches. The hunter of "secret antiques" will have to learn a little about picking locks!

Secret drawers—often cunningly concealed and ingeniously triggered—are far from uncommon in early bureaux and secretaires, according to a leading furniture specialist. "Sometimes the bureau has a central well between the stationery compartments and pigeon holes. If you feel to the right or left you may find concealed drawers. Often, there are carved wooden columns on either side of Georgian mahogany and walnut bureaux and these can be removable and hollow for hiding things in."

What can you hope to find? Personal letters...love tokens...legal documents...jewelery...and so on. Even old deeds — often attractively handwritten on parchment—are collected, and convertible into cash. Why the passion for secrecy? According to the expert, it was a necessity. A servant on a pittance would have no qualms about selling off his master's secrets — if he could get his hands on them.

A mirror is sometimes used to deflect attention and prying fingers (owners of drophead cars use a similar ploy to protect their radios). Antique shipper Ian Butchoff found a nest of drawers behind a mirror in a massive ebony secretaire. Inside were a few papers - nothing to get hot under the collar about. But when he measured the compartment, it was obvious that the drawers were merely a shallow sham, and there was a further cavity behind them. Old gold sovereigns...tie clips...letters and cards bearing valuable stamps and postmarks have all been discovered in secret compartments like that.

Fitted writing slopes—such as might accompany a well-to-do child to boarding school—often have hidey holes. Hold the lid down, give it a good shake, and listen for that tell-tale rattle.

Caxton pages revealed

A bookseller told me about an old volume he had which proved to be worth more when it fell to pieces. Bookbinders used to use broken up old volumes to pad out their own work and brace the spine of new books. This old volume had Caxton pages tucked inside its binding.

Dutch tiles were once all the rage in the UK. But when they went out of favor they were often painted over or a false wall was built over them. And there are many other period features that were similarly covered up as that fashion faded.

A mahogany chest by an unknown maker was recently being photographed. When the drawer was removed a sheet of loose lining paper fell out to reveal a maker's label: Philip Bell, an 18th century craftsman who had his premises in St. Paul's Churchyard, London. Remarkably, a piece by a man who succeeded Mr Bell at that site was later discovered. Another time, a table with a drawer had a broken leg. In fixing it, many years ago, a screw had been driven through the drawer which prevented it being opened. As is often the case with such things, what cannot be used is soon forgotten. Removing the screw and opening the drawer revealed a remarkably well-preserved maker's label: Henry Kettle.

It helps to know where things disappear to in ordinary daily life. I found an old leather case and discovered, trapped beneath the stiffener in the bottom, a silver-on-bronze medallion dated 1830.

Solid silver spoons and valuable old rings have come to light when the drains of an old house are cleaned. Ancient shoe and nail boxes frequently throw up forgotten treasures. Perhaps a gold half-hunter that stopped a hundred years ago or a broken cameo brooch will be yours. And don't overlook the button box. Art Nouveau silver, cloisonné enamel and cut steel varieties may glitter like nuggets among the wood and plastic dross of more recent times.

There's another lead it could pay you to follow. It's an old trick to weight the corners of curtains by sewing a few coins into the hem; old drapes might conceal early coinage in near mint condition.

Pewter—especially early examples without hallmarks or where the mark has disappeared through wear—is occasionally revealed to be silver of fine quality if crude design.

One man bought an old cast iron fender and sold it for a small fortune. He discovered that the piece was solid silver. It had been painted black as a token of respect when Queen Victoria died ...

Broken pieces—especially pottery and ceramics—are generally thought to be lost causes. Often this is not the case. A fine object, carefully repaired and restored, may be worth much more than a perfect but second-rate item.

"Buying a Banjo in London's famous Portobello Road."

12

Collecting For Tomorrow

Miniatures

Many collectors have been scaling down their demands over the years, just in case, in a time of deep recession or even invasion, they ever have to pocket the lot and run! Now what could be more manageably removed than a collection of miniatures?

Souvenir miniatures, like the miniscule books produced by the Black Cat Press, Skokie, Illinois, are in big demand—especially with a pint-sized price tag of $20 to $40 a copy. There are leather-covered, sometimes gold-stamped, and accurately printed versions of everything from Conan Doyle to the Bible; limiting the editions also adds to value. Craftsmanship is the key in miniature book collecting: if you can feel, "Wow! How did they do all that work so small yet so perfectly?", then you are buying right.

Domestic items have always been favorite entities for the scaling down treatment: things like cutlery, pots and pans, glasses and decanters, chairs and tables. One rule of thumb is that whatever would be especially valuable if it were full size becomes enhanced in value when it is conceived as a miniature. Thus a dolls' house chair of impeccable manufacture but tedious shape is nowhere near as entrancing to the collector as a miniature Windsor chair. Tiny tables are fine, but a little marble top Victorian style one is better, while a Louis style table with real miniature ormolu mounts and boulle marquetry is something else. Moving parts are further plus points. A grandfather clock is more exciting if its little pendulum swings. A sewing machine should have a turning wheel for preference. Look, too, for faithfully duplicated locks and hinges.

The first place to look for miniatures is, of course, inside an old dolls' house; the higher the quality of the building generally the better class of furniture you will find inside. But even having spotted a worthy chest or wardrobe there may be further gems inside. A cupboard may reveal a replica Coke bottle fit for a pixie feast, perhaps a ruby goblet or even some of the quarter-inch-high-hand-painted tea sets popular before the last war. Silver cutlery tucked into a kitchen cupboard may be too much to hope for—but keep trying.

Needless to say, there's nothing new about miniatures or collecting them. Spun glass trinkets and toys were made from the 15th century in Europe to be the playthings of the very rich. You won't find many of those about, but 19th century work is still available. Search for glass baskets, decanters, bells, candlesticks, animals and birds. The cruder examples probably were sold at fairs and carnivals. The very best "friggers", as the experts call glass knick-knacks, were made in France. The glassworkers of Nevers made fully-rigged sailing ships with glass sails, hull and the rigging like a spider's web of glass threads. After the mid 19th century cheaper methods of manufacture such as pressing or molding glass enabled many items to be mass-produced. All of the best known UK glass factories of the past contributed miniatures, Nailsea, Bristol, Newcastle and Sunderland among them.

The Steuben Glass Company, famed for its beautiful and delicate glass, also makes delightful miniatures ringing the changes from year to year, so creating rarity value when one line is dropped. *Steuben; Seventy Years of Glassmaking* is a book worth getting from the Toledo Museum of Art, Toledo, Ohio.

Pottery and porcelain miniatures were first introduced from the Orient in the 16th century. Like so many of the earliest miniatures, these bibelots were meant to grace the collectors' cabinets of the gentry. English porcelain is as desirable in miniature as it is in adult-sized crockery. *Crème de la crème* pieces are signed Minton, Coalport, Spode, Worcester; Derby and Worcester, being noted for their candlesticks and candle snuffers. The collecting trick is not to

An Edwardian collection of silver miniatures, marked
Birmingham 1905.

try to get together a complete tea set—even though the cups, saucers, tea pots, etc., were probably issued at once—but to concentrate on cups or tea pots, trying to bring together as many patterns and variations as you can.

Limoges produced lavishly gilded and enamelled wares, while the Scottish varieties of animal and bird shape miniatures with dabbed-on color have become known as "dabbities". Just as Staffordshire flat-backs added sparkle to the dowdy corner of a 19th century cottage, so miniature Staffordshires were made to go in an inglenook of a rustic dolls' house.

One popular fad is reserved strictly for collectors whose own interior decor leaves them something to sing about. They buy miniatures that exactly mirror their own furnishings, then build a tiny room setting in imitation of their room.

Top-of-the-tree miniatures used to be made in silver. Now platinum may be taking over, especially as it is being aggressively promoted as the most precious of all the precious metals, which perhaps prompted one gent to order a Rolls Royce replica from London's Platinum Shop. However, if you're following the rules of this book—and the strictures of your bank manager—you would probably need to invest in a microscope to inspect your platinum collection of miniatures!

There is quite a lot of help to hand for the miniature collector. There's *Miniature Book News,* a periodical, from 16 Dromara, St. Louis, *Books in Bottles,* by Clifford; *Inside World of Minis and Dollshouses,* by Rosner; *Miniature Room Settings,* by Ruthberg; and *One Twelfth,* a guide from Box 107, Norwalk, Connecticut 06856. There is a National Association of Miniature Enthusiasts, Box 2621, Anaheim, California 92804, and a society of Miniaturists, 26 Conduit Street, London W1, England. Barry B. Dobinsky of 1229 Oley Street, Reading, Pennsylvania has fine Pennsylvania miniatures, and more general dealers, like Harvest Country Stores of 1827 Shell Beach Road, California 93449, advertise miniature furniture and baskets. Dealers know that miniatures are a big draw and will get people into their stores.

Miniature books.

If you want to know what is next in line to be collected, there is a short cut that never fails. Read what the pundits of the past had to say: whatever they laughed at is guaranteed to come up trumps tomorrow. In the early Seventies a writer on antiques was decrying a new collectable. In his search for an apogee expression of worthlessness he likened the new fad to a flight of plaster ducks on the wall. He was talking about those gaudily painted models, usually in a range of five, in diminishing size, that flanked our peach mirrors in the Forties and Fifties. Have you tried to buy a set of flying ducks (or geese) recently? You can't get them for love or money. You may find three for $60. But a full set is at a premium. I am convinced that a definitive collection would rate a special event at a leading auction room.

A present-day investment, a print by Richard Kennedy,
"Four Reflections of Virginia."

Another writer talking about country house auctions spoke disparagingly, a few years ago, about the junk end of the range, the woodworking tools you could obtain for next to nothing; useful they certainly could be, but collectable? Never, he implied. And so it was, until Philip Walker and Roy Arnold started to take them seriously in 1974. They issued well-illustrated, meticulously researched catalogs and sold—and bought—through the mails.

Five years later their stock of 6,000-odd items came under the hammer for £62,789 (about $160,000). The latest collectable to be thoroughly disdained is utility furniture issued after the Second World War and into the Fifties. It appears to have no saving grace, its very starkness a harsh reminder of rationing, powdered milk and air raid shelters. But someone, somewhere, sometime is bound to find some merit in it: museums already have. All the old books used to tell us to "buy only what you like": stunted indeed is the collector who needs to like what he buys nowadays. Nor does it help to cast around for remote and unlikely collectables. William Norton has been collecting artificial eyes (wood as well as glass) for the last 60 years; dog collars, plastic giveaways from breakfast food packets have their adherents. Not only is everything collectable, but you can bet your bottom dollar that whatever is remotely conceivable as collectable is *already being collected.*

What can profitably be considered is a new twist to an old theme. Ephemera, paper collectables, are anybody's province. But some modern labels and packaging have a unique reference and the added piquancy of having been produced in limited edition for a tightly controlled market.

Collecting "by the year" has been suggested by Bevis Hillier, former editor of The Connoisseur. He decided on 1874, having bought a child's scrapbook of that date in 1972. In making up his own scrapbook he discovered that 1874 had seen the outbreak of the Ashanti War, that G.K. Chesterton, Somerset Maugham, Gertrude Stein, Houdini and Winston S. Churchill had all been born that year. The possibilities are intriguing. Churchilliana must be a fairly commonplace pursuit, but one might well fix on some more lowly personnage, especially a creative person, and see what might be garnered of their life's work.

Whatever you choose to collect good luck!